THE COMING

THE COMING

A Study in the Christian Faith

by

SISTER PENELOPE, CSMV, S Th

LONDON: A. R. MOWBRAY & CO LTD

Set in 11 on 12 pt Baskerville in Great Britain by
Western Printing Services Ltd, Bristol
and printed and bound in USA

ISBN 0 264 66158 3 (Mowbray)

First published 1974 by
A. R. Mowbray & Co. Ltd,
The Alden Press, Osney Mead, Oxford
and
The Seabury Press
815 Second Avenue
New York, N.Y. 10017

CONTENTS

PART I

PART II

AUTHOR'S NOTE

The two parts of this book were originally published separately: Part I as *The Coming of the Lord* in 1953, and Part II as *As in Adam* in 1954.

Hora novissima,
tempora pessima
sunt;
vigilemus

PART I

INTRODUCTION

THE CREEDS affirm that our Lord Jesus Christ came down from heaven to earth where he was born and died, that he ascended thence to heaven after his Resurrection, and that from heaven he shall come again in glory to judge the living and the dead. But the vision in the Book of Daniel, from which our Saviour took his title 'Son of Man',[1] shows us a single Coming only, the Coming of the 'One like to a Son of Man' to the Ancient of Days in Heaven. And later in the same chapter 'The Man'—for that is what the Aramic *bar-enāsh* denotes—is explained as 'the People of the saints of the Most High'. Thus as there is one only Coming, so also is there the one Man who comes; and our Lord's appropriation of the title shows that we must regard his whole redeeming work as a single movement God- and heavenward. As Dom Gregory Dix put it, 'This is the end and meaning of human history, the bringing of Man, the creature of time, to the Ancient of Days in eternity.'[2]

We may go even further, and point out that the movement that brings Man back to God is itself continuous with the movement of creation. Our Lord says of himself in the Apocalypse 'I am the Alpha and the Omega, the First and the Last, the Beginning and the End.'[3] He, the Creator, is also the Redeemer, the Recreator, and the Consummator; for, as St Athanasius says, only the Word of God, who made all things in the beginning, was both able to recreate all, and worthy to suffer on behalf of all, and to be an ambassador with the Father.[4]

3

Here, however, our concern is only with the movement Godward that is shown in Daniel's vision. In that one Coming, our Lord's two comings down to earth from heaven, and his intermediate ascension from earth into heaven, are incidents. To understand them, we must see them in relation to the whole.

So the theme of this book is that in the Incarnation, in the Spirit, in the Sacraments and in the Judgement, there is a single Coming, and that of Man in his entirety to heaven. It is a vast subject, and only its bare outlines can be indicated here. The approach to it will be a combination of the modern and critical with the traditional and typological. No apology should be required for that; but scholars (if indeed any read the book) must be merciful to its many insufficiently supported statements, as well as to its manifold omissions. It aims only at starting people on a profitable train of thought, and it will fail of its purpose entirely if it does not send them further afield, and above all back to the Bible, to follow it up for themselves. It had to be short.

I

HEAVEN

St Bernard says that, whereas the soul of man was made in the Image of God, his body was fashioned in the image of his soul; and that is why we stand erect. The soul's erectness, however, has been lost by sin; man is now *curvus*, bent, in respect of his spirit, for the Image of God in which it was made is defaced. Of that fact his still upright body reminds him ceaselessly.[1] It seems, moreover, that the body's uprightness has a practical purpose; for it enables him to look forth from the earth and away from himself with an ease unknown to the irrational beasts that go upon all fours. Ex-spectation, therefore, in its literal sense, is a specifically human exercise, something as proper and peculiar to man as are the faculty of speech and the creative use of his hands. And when we exercise our humanness by looking at the sky, what do we see?

We see it arching over all of the earth that we can see; and if we walk right round the earth, the sky is still all over and around. This fact suggests that, if the sky is heaven, earth is itself in heaven and ourselves along with it. There is no getting away from heaven; whether we will or no, we are right in the thick of it, and its eyes are upon us all the time. And yet, though we can see it, we cannot reach or touch it, we cannot go to it, though things from it can come to us on earth. Heaven has then a quality of otherness. And this paradox is unaffected by any degree of scientific knowledge or ignorance about the universe. The Hebrews believed the sky to be a solid dome, holding back the

5

upper waters; they thought that the sun and moon and stars moved about against the under surface of this firmament, and that rain was the upper waters coming through when 'the windows of heaven' were opened. Today we know that this earth is one small planet in one small solar system (relatively speaking), which system is itself only one small member of a vast spiral nebula, that in its turn is only one of at least a hundred billion of such galaxies. But that is only one side of the picture. We also know that, though these heavenly bodies are unimaginable distances apart, they are not only all of them made of the same elements as earth, but they do in literal truth constitute a *universe*, a unity that turns in space as one, the movement of each heavenly dancer determined by and helping to determine that of all the rest. So, willy-nilly, we moderns are still part of heaven; and, equally willy-nilly, it is still beyond our reach.

It is further obvious, when we ex-spect from earth to heaven, that the heat, light, air, and water essential to life on earth all come from it. Man, therefore, though he cannot go to heaven, has to look thither for the means to live, because they simply are not to be had elsewhere. And this obvious physical truth has a spiritual counterpart. Man is a rational animal, built to look forth beyond himself in soul as well as body. So two things happen, when he looks forth humanly to heaven. First, he sees it as the abode of God; and secondly, he finds God's eyes already fixed upon himself. For expectation is reciprocal; God is beforehand with us in that matter, as he is in love. Our power of expectation derives from our creation in his image; our exercise of it is evoked and enabled by his ceaseless looking forth on us.

That, then, is the root of the relation between the sky and God in human thought; and we should not dismiss this basic element of natural religion as something that has no relevance for us today. It is a primitive association, certainly; but things primitive usually have at least a core of something primary, and the principle of the priority of the natural to the spiritual, which St Paul expounds in 1 Cor. 15, is universal and divine. God has always loved the human race and looked forth upon it; and he has never left himself without witnesses. 'He provided the works of creation as means by which the Maker might be known.'[2] The sky is his blackboard; and in the childhood of the race men looked at it with awe and read what he wrote on it readily, even if they sometimes read amiss. Too many people today, if they think about the sky at all, regard it only as a further sphere for human conquest. God is not so much rejected as ignored in the world that he has made, and in his great forbearance still sustains, and an avid pride in what man discovers and achieves has replaced the biblical emphasis on what God reveals and does.

We say at Baptism of the Christian Creed, '*All* this I steadfastly believe'; we are pledged to uphold the whole of the Faith once given to the saints, not merely bits of it. and, as to its terminology, we do well to remember that it is by our Lord's own bidding that we pray, 'Our Father, which *art in heaven*, thy Kingdom *come* in earth, as it *is* in heaven.'[3] Whether it be symbolical or whether it be not, the language is God's choice.

THE COMING TYPIFIED

'I BELIEVE in one God the Father Almighty, Maker of heaven and earth, and of all things visible and invisible.

'And in one Lord Jesus Christ, the Only Begotten Son of God, begotten of his Father before all worlds, God of God, Light of Light, Very God of very God, begotten, not made, being of one substance with the Father, by whom all things were made.

'And I believe in the Holy Spirit, the Lord and the Life-Giver.'[1]

The brief, terrific phrases of the Creed do more than merely put a girdle round the earth; they put a girdle round the universe, and they set time within eternity. The Triune God is Author of it all; it all exists in him, and he in it; that is what makes it holy and symbolic, both as a whole and in its every part. In heaven, seen as other than the earth and yet including and sustaining it, God reveals himself, who is and was and will be, in his relation to mankind. But he reveals his purpose for mankind in man's own history. His blackboard is the sky; to that his children must look up. His sand-tray, on their level where they can poke their fingers in, is the eventful story of his People Israel.

In bringing Man to himself, God uses a selective method to a collective end. The process falls into three parts. The first began with Adam and ended with Abraham; the second began with Abraham and ended with Christ; the third began with Christ, the Second Adam in his single person, and is to end with Christ as Man complete, the

Head and the members in one. Each of these three stages begins with one, expands in the middle to many, and narrows again to one. After Adam comes his fallen and increasing seed, out of which, by way of the remnant saved from the Mesopotamian Flood in the fourth millennium BC, comes Abraham. From Abraham in the second stage proceeds the Chosen People, which narrows to the faithful remnant of the last century BC, that produced Mary of Nazareth and so her Son. From him, the New Man grows into the Church, redeemed mankind, the many who shall be at last One Man in him, and so come to the Father. But all the men that ever were or will be, even our Lord himself, as St Luke is at pains to show,[2] are sons of Adam who was the son of God. It is all one Man, from first to last.

When, therefore, God called Abraham about four thousand years ago to journey to an unknown land, he promised him that in his seed all the families of the earth, Man in his wholeness, should be blessed. That promise, linked at its repetition with the starry sky as a perpetual pledge,[3] ensured that Abraham's seed, when it materialised, should always be a people with a forward look in time as well as space. They would never look back to the Golden Age, as other nations did; they would expect it, in the future. The central complex of events in which God's Plan is outlined is that which begins with Israel's Exodus from Egypt and ends with their re-entrance to their Promised Land. The dates of these events, the location of their sites, the explanation of the phenomena that accompanied them are matters of great interest but very small importance. The facts are the thing; the facts that the children of the Promise, who had become slaves in a foreign land, were first redeemed by sacrifice, then brought out of Egypt through the Sea that drowned their oppressors, then taken into covenant with the God of their fathers, and finally, after a period of wilderness wandering prolonged by their

9

own fault, brought dryshod over Jordan into their own homeland.[4]

The point of the facts is epitomised in the name of the leader who finally led them over. *Joshua* means Yahweh-is-Salvation. The Saviour of Israel was God himself.

No one familiar with the Bible and the liturgy needs to be told that, in these events of the fifteenth or thirteenth century BC, Israel is a type of mankind as a whole, so that their bondage to Pharaoh represents man's to the devil, their wilderness way our earthly pilgrimage, and Canaan, their Promised Land, the heavenly fatherland to which our Jesus-Joshua is bringing us, who is foreshadowed also in the Paschal Lamb, by whose blood in the first place Israel was saved. The thing we are likely to overlook, or to be puzzled by if we do notice it, is the fact that, in this ground-plan of God's redeeming, recreating Work, there is no incident to correspond either to his first Coming, or to his Ascension, or to his Return to earth. The Incarnation as a whole is adumbrated by the Lord's repeatedly expressed intention to 'dwell among' his people;[5] and that he did indeed so dwell was represented to them by the Ark and Tabernacle, and the Shekinah that appeared before it; but symbols corresponding to the From, Into, and Thence of the Creeds are entirely lacking. This is a fact of great significance. The ground-plan of God's Work thus outlined in the sand of Israel's history shows it in outline only, as the single movement of his bringing of Man to himself. The Bible story emphasises that. It begins with 'Let My People *go*'—that is, go home, where they belong. And by sacrifice and Sea, by Sinai and the wilderness and over Jordan river, home they go. The movement is from earth to heaven all along. Christ's to and fro-ing between heaven and earth subserves that single Coming of Mankind to God.

We saw just now that the Exodus story was the central

complex of events in which the ground-plan of God's saving Work was typified. It is central in importance, for nowhere else even in Israel's history are the outlines of that Work so clear; and it is central also in respect of time. For, if you read the Old Testament carefully, you find that the People of God themselves regarded the Great Deliverance from Egypt as an Act of God on a pattern already revealed; and you find also that, in course of time, they came to expect a third and similar, yet greater, Act to follow. The archetype is the Creation story. The Genesis account of the world's beginning is a late, sublimated form of an ancient polytheistic myth which the Hebrews shared with their Mesopotamian neighbours; but in other parts of the Old Testament the same myth appears in a much earlier and cruder form. In Isa. 51.9 and 51.10, for instance, the Revised Standard Version reads:

Awake, awake, put on strength, O arm of the Lord;
    awake as in the days of old,
    the generations of long ago.
Was it not thou that didst cut Rahab in pieces,
    that did pierce the dragon?
Was it not thou that didst dry up the sea,
    the waters of the great deep,
that didst make the depths of the sea a way
    for the redeemed to pass over?

The reference to the Exodus is obvious; so also is the expectation of a new deliverance; we shall return to that in the next chapter. But if you read the passage in Hebrew, something more appears. 'The Lord' of course is Yahweh, he who was and is and will be, and the meaning would be clearer if we rendered, 'Art thou not *he who*' did all these things. Further, not Rahab only but Dragon and Sea and Great Deep are all of them proper names. Tannîn, Yām and Tehôm Rabbāh. The first three names—Rahab means 'Stormy One'—are variants for the fourth, Tehôm. In the Babylonian form of the Creation myth, the two primeval monsters were Apsû and Tiâmât, Abyss and Deep; when their waters mingled, then the gods arose; and when the parents turned against their progeny, the god who finally slew Tiâmât, when all the rest had failed, was Mardûk, the Sun-god; he 'cleft her like a flatfish in two parts', from one of which he made the firmament and from the other the dry land, to be the home of Man. Here in the Hebrew version Tehôm is one in name and character with Tiâmât,[6] the Enemy; Yahweh takes Mardûk's place as Hero-God, 'cuts Rahab', and dries up Sea. And in Ps. 136.13 it is he also who 'divided Yam Sūph (Red Sea) in two parts', and made Israel to go through its midst. The issue of the conflict with the Enemy in the first Act of God was the establishment of Man on the stable earth. The issue in the second was the formation of his Chosen People and their establishment in Canaan. Both saving acts were equally historical to the Hebrew mind; they followed the same pattern, because the same God brought them to pass.

3

THE COMING PROPHESIED

THE centuries following the Settlement in Canaan saw some great changes in the circumstances of the Chosen People. They, who had been shepherds only, became settled farmers too. They acquired the kingship, so that henceforward God's Presence in their midst was symbolised by the sacred person of the king, as well as by the Ark. And finally Jerusalem, the ancient seat of the priest-kings 'after the order of Melchizedek' of the Sun-god Elyôn, became their royal and their holy city, where the stone Temple replaced the tabernacle as the shrine of the Ark.

These changes influenced their expectation and their thought in several ways. They were still God's People Israel, in whom he willed to dwell; and they were still the seed of Abraham, through whom the Lord had promised to bless all mankind. But almost from the foundation of the monarchy the hope for the future began to be focused on the royal line. This comes out most strikingly in 2 Sam. 7, a chapter to read and re-read, for it is one of the key passages in Holy Scripture. David, having made Jerusalem his capital, desires to make it further the Lord's holy city by building him a stone House to contain the Ark. In a message by the prophet Nathan, God tells the king three things: first, that he has 'walked in a tent' since the Exodus and never asked for an House, with the implication that there is no hurry now; then *that he himself will make a House for David*; and lastly, that David's peaceful son shall build the House of the Lord that David may not build himself. All through the chapter the two Houses, the man-built lifeless Temple and the God-given human royal family, weave in and out; from this source springs the Messianic Hope. Further, by the end of the pre-exilic period experience and environment had given Israel four main analogies for her relationship with God. First and foremost he was her Shepherd, who had led her out of Egypt. Then he was her Inhabitant, dwelling in her midst. Thirdly, by the sublimation of a Canaanite conception, he was her loving Husband, the source of her fertility, and outraged by her going after other gods. Lastly, he was her King. We shall return to these analogies in Chapter 5. We pass on now to the situation which gave rise to that hope of a new Act of God, a further Great Deliverance, to which we referred at the end of Chapter 2.

The earliest writing prophets had foretold the Exile as the inevitable doom on national apostasy; but they—and Jeremiah too, who saw it happen—foretold also that a faithful remnant would return. One of that purged and godly company in Babylon round about 540 BC was the prophet commonly called the Second Isaiah. The power of Babylon was declining, the power of Persia rising; it looked as though the fall of Babylon might bring liberation to the Jews. There, then, from the point of view of the faithful exiles, was the quite glorious opportunity for the Lord God to effect another and a greater Exodus and once again to bring his People home. To that the prophet urged him in the passage cited from Isa. 51. In the next chapter, verses 1 to 12, the theme is expanded to show the route of the new Exodus from either end. First we see Jerusalem, the desecrated and despoiled, bidden to arise from the dust; then we are shown the ransomed host, whom God is leading home from Babylon, already started on their wilderness way. Nor is this all. The gap is closed, the Road is unified, before our eyes. Someone, a Bringer of Good News, runs on ahead, up the Judaean hills, to tell Jerusalem, 'Thy God has become King!'

Such is the hope in this and other passages of Second Isaiah.[1] But the actual Return in 535 BC was in glaring contrast with these glowing prophecies. The band of exiles, whom Zerubbabel the prince and Jeshua the priest led back, was but a fraction of the people; no portents marked their journey and, when they reached their desolated country, life was intolerably hard. The restoration of the Temple, though begun immediately, was soon allowed to lapse; and even when after some sixteen years it was resumed, it was a poor affair compared with Solomon's. Nor was that all. The returned People lacked both the former symbols of God's Presence in their midst; the Ark was lost, and the Davidic monarchy was not restored.

This bleak and bitter difference between the prophecies and the event has led to the suggestion[2] that God may have meant the Incarnation to take place immediately upon the Jews' return, but that the human agent of his choice did not respond. If that were so, those last five centuries before the Advent, waiting for Mary of Nazareth to come and say, 'Behold, the handmaid of the Lord!', are rather like the extra forty years that Israel wandered in the wilderness, because they lacked the faith and courage to proceed at once. But however this may have been, the contrast between expectation and fulfilment does not mean that the prophet was mistaken in foretelling a great new Act of God. It only means that he was seeing double—seeing two things, yet seeing them as one.

There has been a good deal about seeing double in this book already, although we have not previously called it by that name. The universe is sacramental, because God is in it; we ourselves are double, being body and soul, and we are always using symbolical and metaphorical language. A symbol is literally something thrown together; and the togetherness implies two elements. The word is used in two distinct although related senses. Baptismal Creeds are called symbols, because they stand for the faith of those who recite them and so distinguish Christians from non-Christians. The Union Jack and the old school tie are similarly symbols of particular loyalties; and the dinner-bell is a symbol that the meal is ready. In symbols of this kind, the thing seen or heard represents certain ideas but does not resemble them. In symbols of the other kind, however, the two things thrown together are alike. That is why we called the story of the Deliverance from Egypt the ground-plan of God's Work; because the elements in that story are like the elements in the deliverance of man from his enemy the devil, though on a different plane. And it is only by such analogies that we can apprehend spiritual things and realities beyond our present experience at all. As every teacher knows, when you want to teach your pupils something new, you must begin with something they already know quite well. The ladder that is to reach to heaven must have its feet on earth.

Prophetic double vision follows the same principle. The famous passage in Isa. 7.1–17 is an example. When Ahaz of Judah, set on alliance with Assyria against Israel and Syria despite Isaiah's contrary advice, refuses to ask God for a sign that Judah has nothing to fear from those two countries, Isaiah replies that the Lord himself will give the king a sign of the folly of the course on which he has determined; the '*almah*,[3] he says, shall conceive and bear a son, and before the child is old enough to know good from evil, Judah, as well as Israel and Syria, will have been laid waste. That is the immediate prophecy; for '*almah* is the common word for any young woman of marriageable age, and the promised child may have been one of Ahaz' own.

But '*almah* can also mean a maiden not yet married, and so it covers the second thing within the prophet's vision, Messiah's virgin birth. The first Isaiah, therefore, sees two future happenings, one near and one remote; one of such transitory import that today we do not know just how it came about; the other no less than the Incarnation of the Son of God. So is it also with the Second Isaiah. He foresees the historical Return of the Jews to Jerusalem; and in and beyond that he sees the End to which all history leads, the ultimate Coming of Man, in Christ, to God.

That is prophetic double vision; and these prophecies of Second Isaiah are the very peak of Hebrew prophecy because in them, as from a mountain top, the seer looks across those disappointed yet expectant centuries, to the Coming of God in the flesh and the potential consummation of his saving work on Calvary. For we owe this nameless prophet more than the prophecies of the Return, that tell of the Voice crying for the homeward road to be prepared and of the Bringer of Good News to Sion, who is the first to tread that holy road from end to end; we owe him also the four songs about the Suffering Servant of the Lord, sent, obedient, rejected, led as a lamb to the slaughter, yet by his willing death saving the very people who do away with him.[4] And here is a strange thing. The Book of Isaiah is a compilation; and even the chapters assigned to our prophet are patently a patchwork of separate oracles. But the supreme vision of the Return to Jerusalem, which includes the figure of the Forerunner who brings her the Good News, is in chapter 52, verses 1–12; and the supreme vision of the Servant who effects salvation by his willing death follows immediately in 52.13 to the end of 53. They are not joined, they are just laid alongside. Nothing, except their juxtaposition, suggests that the two figures are the same. Neither is there any indication as to who the Servant is, save that 'Servant of

17

the Lord' is a royal title, and is equated with Messiah in Ps. 89.

Let us look again at this thrice-drawn pattern of the Act of God.

In the Creation myth, he conquers Chaos (Great Tehôm) and makes heaven and earth out of her, earth being fashioned for the home of man.

In the Exodus story, he conquers Egypt, makes Red Sea a way for the ransomed (that is, Israel redeemed by the sacrifice of the lamb) to pass over. He then recreates them as the Covenant People and, by the hand first of Moses and then of Joshua, leads them home to Canaan.

In Second Isaiah, he conquers Babylon (by the hand of Cyrus), delivers his People from her, and brings them home to Jerusalem.

This he does as King. A forerunner brings Jerusalem the good news of her children's approaching return. Sacrifice does not enter directly into this third picture; but in the companion vision the royal Suffering Servant of the Lord is led as a lamb to the slaughter and saves his People by his willing death.

Thus all the salient features of the Creation and the Exodus reappear in the Second Isaiah, but with him the plan is drawn in finer lines and with development. The fact that now Jerusalem, the Holy City, is the specific goal of the Return, not just the Holy Land in general, is interesting. The theocratic city-state, such as Jerusalem ideally was, was a Sumerian invention, with which the father of the faithful must have been familiar in Ur and Harran, a thousand years before the Greeks evolved their city-states or his own seed came to Jerusalem. Such cities centred on the temple, that was the House of God; and the Return that Second Isaiah sees is God's to his own place, as well as the people's to theirs. The prophet, moreover, sees the great event as a meeting of heaven and earth. 'Drop down, ye heavens, from above,' he cries in another passage, 'and let the earth open and bring forth salvation!'[5]

4

ON INSPIRATION AND
BELIEVING IN THE
HOLY SPIRIT

ST MARK, the earliest evangelist, derives his title, *The Good News of Jesus Christ*, from the Greek version of the passage in Isa. 52 about the Bringer of Good News to Sion;[1] he further prefaces his story with a conflation of another passage from the Second Isaiah with one from post-exilic Malachi.[2] St Matthew likewise sees the Baptist as the Voice which, in Isa. 40, cries for the holy road to be made ready for the Lord; St Luke at the same point echoes or quotes four or five other passages from Second Isaiah as well.[3] The peak of prophecy is thus the starting-point of the New Testament; and the Synoptists' approach is underpinned by that of the Fourth Evangelist who, going back still further, sees the beginning of a new Creation in the Incarnation of the Word of God, who was in the beginning and by whom all things were made.[4] But before we proceed to the New Testament, let us clear our minds on the subject of Inspiration.

The Hebrew word for truth, *'eméth*, has the root meaning of that on which you can depend. God's truth is thus his faithfulness. Our Lord said of himself, 'I am the Truth,' and of the Holy Spirit, 'He shall guide you into all the truth.'[5] We say in the Nicene Creed that we believe in the Holy Spirit, who spake by the prophets. 'The prophets' covers all the Scriptural forthtellers of his word under both covenants; and to believe *in* means to trust. That the Spirit spoke by the prophets is of faith; it is not of faith that he speaks by the critics, though he may do so. This statement intends no disrespect towards the scholars who in the last three generations have laboured in the Biblical field with such devotion and often with such rich result. It simply points a distinction that is often overlooked. The Scriptures have the *nihil obstat* of the undivided Church of the first centuries; the Spirit who guided the writers guided the selection of the writings too. Because he never overrides his human agents, 'the prophets', though inspired, sometimes made mistakes. But the Inspirer is himself the guarantee that these mistakes are such as do not matter, and that the substance of their message, often so far transcending what they knew, is utterly dependable and true. For instance, the author of the Book of Daniel believed that the Medes and the Persians were two separate and consecutive powers; so when he saw a vision of four empires successively oppressing the Jews, he called them the Chaldaeans, the Medes, the Persians, and the Greeks, the Greek oppression being at its height in his own day. In point of fact, the Medes and the Persians were one; so the Greek domination was only the third. But the Roman was to follow, though the prophet did not know it; and, when the Jews were under Roman rule, his prophecy of salvation under the fourth empire was fulfilled in Christ. Again, St Luke has been criticised for speaking of a census 'over all the world' at the time of our Lord's birth, and of a similarly universal famine at the end of Acts 11, neither of which is recorded in contemporary history. This seems to be due to the fact that he was ignorant of Palestinian Aramaic, though he knew the Syrian dialect.[6] In these two passages his Aramaic sources gave him the word *'arçah*, which had in Palestine, besides the general meaning 'earth' or 'land', the special meaning of 'The Land', the

Holy Land itself. Misunderstandings such as that hurt nobody. But if you believe in the Holy Spirit and that he spake by the prophets, you *cannot* believe that Holy Scripture contains serious error, whatever the critics may say. In Chapter 7 we shall have to consider some specific instances of such suggestions; for the present, we shall go forward to the New Testament, serenely convinced that whatever we find there is put there for our learning and has, if one may use the term, been passed by God.

5

FROM HEAVEN: INTO HEAVEN

St Matthew and St Luke, as has been said, follow St
Mark in representing the mission of the Baptist and the
ensuing ministry of Jesus as the true fulfilment of the
Second Isaiah's prophecies of the Return to Jerusalem,
that had failed so signally of realisation in the events of
Jewish history five centuries before. But they do not begin
with that. They preface the Marcan Gospel with accounts
of how the Lord in the first place 'came down from heaven,
and was incarnate by the Holy Spirit of the Virgin Mary,
and was made man'.[1]

Consider how first one and then the other of these
evangelists stresses the fact that, in the Son of Mary, God
has indeed rent the heavens and come down. An angel is
sent from heaven to tell the chosen daughter of the House
of David what God wills to do, as earlier he had told the
father of the Lord's forerunner. An angel in a dream ex-
plains to Joseph how Mary comes to be with child and who
that Child shall be; an angel announces his birth to the
Bethlehem shepherds, and is thereupon joined by a host of
his fellows, singing glory to God in high heaven and peace
to men on earth whose wills are set aright. A star in heaven
guides the Gentile sages to the child who is born the King
of the Jews. And, with all that, the sheer hard fact that
there was no room in the inn at David's Bethlehem, in
which the mother of Messiah might give birth to him,
denotes the wider tragedy that, when God came from
heaven to his own on earth, his own received him not.[2]

23

The fact that this event at the outset of his life is typical of something bigger than itself should prepare us to see types in other incidents of our Lord's earthly life; indeed, he can hardly open his lips or move in the Gospel story without either fulfilling prophecy or setting forth in some way what he had come from heaven to earth to do; and his miracles are as significant in this respect as are his parables. In Chapter 3 we said that, after Israel became a settled and a king-ruled people, she had four main analogies for her relationship with God; he was her Shepherd, her Inhabitant, her Husband, and her King. Let us briefly follow those four figures in the life of Jesus, and see what light they throw upon the purpose of his coming down to earth.

The chief Shepherd passages are the Parable of the Lost Sheep in Luke 15.3–7 and Matt. 18.12–14 and our Lord's description of himself as the Good Shepherd in John 10.1–18. The former is spoken to the Pharisees, who were shocked at his mixing with sinners. The point of it is that the one *lost* sheep is so precious to its owner, that without hesitation he leaves the ninety and nine and goes in search of it; its value is further emphasised by the general joy when he brings it safely home. The context shows that the immediate reference is individual; the lost sheep is the sinful soul. But the Fathers interpret the lost sheep as meaning Man, and the ninety and nine as the unfallen angels who rejoice in heaven when Christ brings the lost one home, and so completes their number. It is deeply significant also that in Luke 19.10, when our Lord is again criticised for consorting with a 'sinner', he replies that *the Son of Man* has come to seek and save the lost—the Son of Man, The Man, who in Dan. 7 is explained as meaning 'the saints of the Most High', and comes and is brought to the Ancient of Days in heaven.

In the Good Shepherd passage, the lost sheep is a flock,

subject to hostile and thievish depredations. The emphasis is on the Shepherd's unremitting care and service of the flock, his personal relationship with every sheep in it, and finally upon the fact that he gives his own life that the sheep may live. It thus recalls two separate visions of the Second Isaiah, that of God as Shepherd tenderly leading his ransomed People home in chapter 40, and that of the Suffering Servant of the Lord, who in chapter 53 effects that redemption by giving his own life in sacrifice. 'A Lamb the sheep hath ransomed', as the Easter sequence says.

The idea of God as Inhabitant, Indweller in mankind, underlies the little parable of the Strong Man and the Stronger. Our Lord gave utterance to it when he, in whom dwelt all the fulness of the Godhead bodily, had been accused of casting out the devils by the power of their prince. It is a picture very broadly drawn, with little detail. The Strong Man, fully armed, is in secure possession of the house, *until* the Stronger comes, takes from him all the weapons on which he counted for maintaining it, and divides the spoils.[3] The two characters, the Strong and the Stronger than he, recall the classic tale of David vanquishing Goliath and cutting off his head with his own sword;[4] but here the Strong is in possession of a *house*— and is turned out of it. Our Lord had just been casting devils out of people; as in the Parable of the Lost Sheep and in the healing miracles, the individual application precedes and typifies the general. For it is *Man*, created for Divine indwelling, who is enemy-occupied; and the Son of David, the Stronger than the Strong, has come to wrest from the usurping foe his trusted weapons of suffering and death, and restore the house to its owner.

Plainer than any parable, however, to declare this theme were his symbolic actions. Twice, if we take the Gospels as they stand, he ejected from that new and lovely Temple at Jerusalem those who were using it for alien purposes. The

25

first occasion, recorded in John 2.13–22, was at Passover, soon after he began his ministry; the disciples were reminded by that fierce effective anger of the words of Psalm 49, 'The zeal of thine House shall eat me up.' And, when the Jews asked him what sign he showed, that he acted thus, he answered, 'Destroy this Temple, and in three days I will raise it up.' His words were received with derision; but, says the evangelist, looking back on the scene in the light of the Resurrection, '*He spake of the temple of his Body.*' Jesus was never forgiven for that Temple saying; the Synoptists, who do not record its origin, tell how he was reproached with it, of course in twisted form, while the destruction of the temple of his Body was in process on the Cross. It is the Synoptists also who give the story of the second Cleansing, again at Passover, within a few days of his death. It appears as the climax of his triumphal entry into Jerusalem, which we shall come to later, in connection with the thought of God as King. But we may note in passing that, on this occasion, Jesus conflates two sayings from the prophets to support his action. 'Is it not written, my House shall be called the house of prayer for all nations? But ye have made it a den of robbers' (Isa. 56.7, Jer. 7.11).

The figure of God as Husband of his people, of which Hosea, Jeremiah, and the Second Isaiah had treated,[5] is changed in the New Testament, and the change is most deeply significant. Our Lord spoke of himself not as the husband but as the *bridegroom*.[6] He spoke one parable about the marriage-feast of a king's son, to which the guests invited failed to come; and another about ten virgins waiting to be called to a marriage, of whom only half were ready when at last the bridegroom came. Except for the saying of John the Baptist, 'He that hath the bride is the bridegroom', the bride is never mentioned in the Gospels. Why? Surely because she did not yet exist, because the

New Eve had yet to be created, as the Fathers loved to say, out of the pierced side of the Second Adam on the Cross.[7] Later in the New Testament St Paul in Eph. 5.22ff., uses the husband and wife analogy for the relation between Christ and his Church, but does not expressly name her either wife or bride. In the Apocalypse, however, right to the end she is only the bride, the wife to be. For the Church is not yet wholly one with Christ, as man was one with God before the Fall; and the consummation of 'the marriage of the Lamb' with the bride of his own redeeming and re-making is itself the consummation for which the whole creation waits.[8]

Our Lord, then, represented the Work that he came down from heaven to do under three homely human meta-phors. He came as Shepherd, to find the one lost sheep and take it home and, in the process, give his life for it. He came as Son of the Owner of the House, to conquer and evict the thief. He came as Bridegroom, to win his bride and unite her to himself. And over and above all these he came as King.

The thought of God as King is dominant in the Old Testament; but in this case the metaphor appears to be reversed. For it is not so much that human kingship is pro-jected on to God, as that God's Kingship is reflected in that of his human vicegerent, who sits uplifted on his earthly throne only because God, whom he serves and represents, reigns in the height of heaven. The ritual pattern of the king-ruled peoples who were Israel's neighbours included a Divine Accession Feast, in which the deity, in the person of his human vicegerent, mounted his throne anew and so inaugurated the New Year, and having thus taken his power anew, proceeded to exercise judgement, bestowing reward or punishment according to deserts. There is some evidence that, before the Exile, the Chosen People also kept this Divine Accession Feast, this 'Day of the Lord', as part of the great autumn Feast of Tabernacles. But whether they kept the Feast or not, the Old Testament shows that they were wholly familiar not only with all the ideas embodied in the Feast but also with some at least of its ritual concomitants, such as the cry, 'Yahweh has become King!' the blowing of the sacred ram's horn, and the clapping of hands. The same thought-circle, with the same horn-blowing, persists in the Synagogue liturgy for the New Year Feast today. And in the New Testament it is so prominent that one may dare to say it has provided the framework for the Christian Creed.

In the time of Christ, the Messianic Hope existed in two forms. There was the prophetic hope of the restoration of the House and Throne of David; and there was the apocalyptic hope of a sublimated king, such as the mysterious Son of Man. The former hope was temporal, even political, the prince of the blood might be expected to lead a revolution and free the Jews from Roman domination. The latter hope was supra-temporal and other-worldly. In the Infancy stories, as we saw, our Lord is clearly the Davidic king of prophecy. But then he disappears for thirty years and, when the Baptist heralds his return and he himself begins his ministry, the emphasis is on the Kingdom, not the king. 'The Kingdom, the Reign of God has come!' That is the Good News, as it was in Isa. 52; God has become King, has assumed his power. Thereafter our Lord speaks parable after parable about the Kingdom of Heaven or of God; paradoxically he adduces his own miracles as proof that it *has* come and teaches his followers to pray that it *may* come, on earth as it is in heaven. But he eludes popular attempts to make him king, and the sole title that he uses of himself is Son of Man. He clearly shows himself as King, God's Agent for establishing his Rule on earth, only in two tremendous acts, his solemn entry into Jerusalem five days before his death, and his ascension into heaven after he had risen.[9]

There is so much that is obvious about Palm Sunday, our Lord's deliberate and literal fulfilment of Zechariah's prophecy about the peaceful king, the bitter contrast between that triumph and the Passion following, that other things no less significant often get overlooked. For instance, a procession with branches and Ps. 118 was a feature of the Feast of Tabernacles which, as we said just now, was also the Feast of New Year and full of the thought of God's Kingship; and the goal of that procession was the Temple altar, the place of sacrifice. So that impromptu procession of Passover pilgrims on the first Palm Sunday combined the themes and types of both those two great Feasts. But over and above all that, the festal coming of Christ to Jerusalem was a symbol of his final, finished Coming to the Father as the Son of Man. That, at least, is how St Bernard sees it. The liturgical palm procession, he says, which re-enacts that entry, represents the glory of our heavenly fatherland. As we walk in it, we should think what joy will be ours when we are caught up to meet Christ in the air, and we should long with our whole heart to see that Day when Christ the Lord, the Head with all his members, shall be received into the heavenly Jerusalem, bearing the palm of victory and with angelic powers and the peoples of both testaments crying on every side, 'Blesséd is he who comes in the Name of the Lord!' That is your goal, he says; and the Passion, read in the Mass that follows the procession, shows you the road that you must take to reach it.[10]

So the symbolism of the Triumphal Entry looks beyond his even more triumphant Ascension into heaven from the Mount of Olives a few weeks later. It sees the King, the Man who then rode solitary to his willing death and later went alone to heaven, leaving his friends on earth, ascending to his Father finally, together with redeemed, remade mankind, his Bride the Church. What, then, does the Ascension mean, and how does it fit in?

Between Christ's first descent from heaven to earth and his ascension thither from the Mount of Olives, he died and rose again. And, as that complex of events, from his conception as Man to his ascension in that same humanity to heaven, is the heart and centre of the whole movement of salvation, so is the Sixth Word from the Cross the centre of that centre, the point to which all leads and from which all proceeds. *Tetélestai*. It is finished.[11] It has been consummated, perfected. The Aramaic Perfect, which our Lord must have used, conveys just that: the Work is done. But the Greek Perfect that translates it brings out more, for it implies that the results of the thing done are still going on. By the sacrificial Death of Christ as Man for man, the Work of Creation itself, as well as of Redemption, was then and there potentially made perfect. The Death itself, as the Fourth Evangelist so clearly sees, was the triumph and the glory; only the demonstration of the triumph, the visible vindication by the Lord God of his anointed Son, was delayed till the third day. And just as the Death and Resurrection are in this sense one thing, so also are the Resurrection and Ascension one, separated in time only for the sake of those for whose salvation he had in the first place come down from heaven.

The Ascension, then, embodies the same paradox as the Sixth Word. The triumph is complete, potentially. In terms of the old analogies, Joshua comes home across the river and the Forerunner of the exiles reaches Jerusalem; he comes alone, but his coming is the pledge that Man shall follow. And under this last figure it is good to think of the Ascension from the Jerusalem end, to think of the joy of the inhabitants of heaven at receiving Perfect Man at last among them, in the Person of the Son of God, and at

30

the prospect of presently receiving all mankind. Indeed, if from the point of view of earth the two foci of the ellipse of our Lord's one Coming to the Father are his two descents to earth, may we not think that, from the point of view of heaven, the foci are his two ascents, the first when he returned alone as Man, the second when, after his second descent, he returns finally with all redeemed mankind? At all events, it is good to remember sometimes that heaven has a point of view, and takes an interest in earth.

Our Lord's Ascension is also his accession to the throne of God. Taking his royal power, he brings in the New Age, bestows the Holy Spirit as his gift for men, judges, though not yet openly, expects till all his enemies on earth be overcome. All that he does as King. As Shepherd, he goes before his flock to lead the way; as the Ark of God's Indwelling, he is uplifted to his resting-place; as Bridegroom, he goes to prepare a place for his Bride. Whichever way you look at it, the Ascension from the Mount of Olives, tremendous, glorious climax though it is, is only a point in the curve, a stage in his one Coming to the Father, not its consummation, though it prefigures it. We pray in the Collect for Ascension Day that we may in heart and mind thither ascend, whither our Saviour Christ is gone before. That, for the present, is all that we can do. But let us not forget that we are destined eventually to ascend to heaven in our bodies, our final, risen bodies, too.

6

THESE LAST DAYS

'But when Christ had offered for all time a single sacrifice for sins, he sat down at the right hand of God, then to wait until his enemies should be made a stool for his feet. For by a single offering he has perfected for all time those who are sanctified.'[1]

That is how the author of Hebrews sums up the paradox of the Sixth Word, using the perfect tense of an almost identical verb for 'he has perfected.' It is all done, the Work of our salvation; yet it is still to do; and both the great analogies confirm the fact. Israel, redeemed from Egypt and admitted to the Covenant, has still to travel through the wilderness for forty years before she can cross Jordan and come home. The exiles, freed at last and setting out from Babylon, have seven hundred miles of wilderness to traverse before they reach Mount Zion. Both types imply a long and toilsome way. And both apply to Man redeemed in Christ, and not only to individual men; indeed, they mean the part only because they first denote the whole. You and I will 'cross the river' when we die; but that does not exhaust the meaning of the type, nor is our personal crossing a completed thing. Rather, it is itself a type and pledge of the great final Crossing of the human race. Men die; and so must the one Man, some day. For the New Man Christ Jesus, by his own willing death, has made death the way to life for the race, as well as for the individual.

Meanwhile, the wilderness way for all of us. And what exactly is the function of that discipline?

It is to afford Man in Christ the opportunity to share Christ's human experience from Bethlehem to Calvary inclusive, so that at the end of these Last Days he may be brought thence to the glory of his Resurrection and the everlasting Life. In the arena of this present life, Man's business is to work out his own salvation,[2] to make his own what Christ has done for him; though paradoxically it is of course still Christ who works out his salvation in him—Christ who is with us all the days, even to the end of the Age,[3] for all he is in heaven and unseen. In the Church his Body he extends his Incarnation, giving to each of his members the opportunity and power to share his saving life and death and so, eventually, to share his Resurrection and Ascension too. Of all the New Testament writers, St Paul puts this best. 'It is now my happiness to suffer for you', he says. 'This is my way of helping to complete, in my poor human flesh, the full tale of Christ's afflictions still to be endured, for the sake of his Body, which is the Church.'[4] The afflictions of Christ that have still to be suffered and offered and done, that the all-sufficient sacrifice may be completed—there is the paradox of the Sixth Word again.

That filling up is the whole business of these Last Days, this final Age of human history, that came in with the Incarnation and in which we live. That is the stuff of Christian life, that is the process, plain to the sympathetic eyes of heaven[5] but mostly hidden from our human view, that all the sacraments and means of grace subserve.

7

THENCE HE SHALL COME

HE 'came down from heaven', and 'ascended into heaven' in the past. 'He sits at the right hand of the Father' now. Thence, at the end of these Last Days, 'he shall come again with glory to judge both the quick and the dead, whose kingdom shall have no end.'

That is the faith which we Christians are pledged to hold and to hand on in its integrity. Why is it that we hear and read so little about the future part?

The trouble starts from the fact that the promise of our Lord's Return was given nearly two thousand years ago, and still he has not come. Delay (as it appears) has generated doubt. Because some, at any rate, of the first generation of Christians looked for him to come in their own lifetime, the idea has grown up that perhaps the Church herself was mistaken in expecting his Return at all. Such a notion, if it were valid, would—as we tried to show in Chapter 4—make Inspiration meaningless. If you believe in the Holy Spirit, you must accept the future Second Coming of our Lord as just as integral a part of the faith once delivered to the saints as is the First.

I have put this strongly, because it is a matter on which there is great need for us to clear our minds and have the courage of our faith. Let us now examine the grounds on which this theory of error rests.

The first is the fact that, all through the New Testament, the Messianic Age is regarded as having already begun.[1] The second is ultimately none other than the passage in

Dan. 7 on which—though with a difference—this present book is based. For it is argued that, when our Lord said to Caiaphas, 'You shall see the Son of Man sitting at the right hand of power and coming on the clouds of heaven', which is a patent reminiscence of Daniel's Son of Man, he was referring not to his coming again *to earth* but to his coming to *heaven*. That prophecy (they say) was fulfilled at the Ascension, the Last Things, therefore, have already come. But the early Church misunderstood his words and so, by wishful thinking—and how should they not wish?— arose the notion that he would return. But this 'realised eschatology' is only half the truth, half of the paradox of the Sixth Word. The Ascension from the Mount of Olives was an incident prefiguring the final consummation, not the End itself. Like the Sixth Word, Christ's words to Caiaphas show how, in his Passion, he was ex-specting to that final End, his ultimate and perfect Coming to the Father as the Head with the Body, the Bridegroom with the Bride. 'Jesus', says Hebrews, 'who, for the sake of the joy that lay ahead of him endured the cross, making light of its disgrace.'[2]

But his fullest expectation to that blesséd End is in the thirteenth chapter of St Mark. Observe its setting, both in time and place. It is Tuesday evening in Holy Week. As Jesus and the disciples pass the Temple on their way back to Bethany, one of them points to it. Our Lord replies that it is going to be entirely destroyed. They go on down into the Kidron valley, thinking about that, and up the other side. There, on the western flank of Olivet, 'over against the Temple', they sit down. It looms in front of them against the evening sky. Then four disciples ask him privately to tell them when his prophecy will be fulfilled and by what sign fulfilment will be heralded. *The Temple*, that only yesterday, according to St Mark, Jesus had so significantly cleansed, is the matter in hand as well as the

35

object in view; *and the Temple is a type of Man, created for God's Indwelling.*

In Chapter 3 we spoke about prophetic double vision. The prophets in the examples cited may or may not have realised that they were seeing two things, and not only one; in any case, they could not clearly differentiate between them. But here, in Mark 13, the Prophet of prophets is speaking, to whom the Spirit was not given by measure; he sees two things, and keeps the two entirely distinct. Both things are Ends—the End of the Temple first, that is of the type; and then the End of Man, whom the Temple typifies.

And let us be quite certain what we mean by End. There are two words for End in the Greek Testament, *telos* and *synteleia*; and they are both from the same stem as the two almost identical verbs which gave us respectively our Lord's *Tetélestai* and the *teteleiōken* of Heb. 10.14, quoted on page 34. The root idea is therefore positive, not negative; the end of a thing is the purpose for which it exists. 'When a smith says of a sword, "It is finished", he means that it is ready to be used.'³ Only when it has served its purpose and has no longer any *raison d'être*, does the end of a thing mean its ceasing to exist. The two Ends that our Lord is seeing in Mark 13 exactly illustrate this difference. The End of the Temple was the destruction of the Temple, because the type was no longer needed when the thing typified, the New Humanity, had come. But when Man comes to his End, he will be finished in the sense of being ready, at last, for the purpose for which he was made.

Let us now look at the discourse which answers the disciples' question. Verses 5 to 23 are a straightforward statement as to what they must expect in their own lifetime. 'The beginning of travail' will be false teaching, wars, earthquakes, and famines. They themselves will be persecuted and betrayed and hated for his sake; but they are to flee from Judaea only when they see the Temple profaned, for so would any Jew, remembering the profanation by Antiochus, understand verse 14. And all that was fulfilled within just over forty years; the year 71 saw the End of the Temple, and the Jerusalem Church had obediently made its escape to Pella before the End took place.

In verse 24 our Lord passes from the type to the thing typified. The transition is marked first by the adversative conjunction 'but', implying that these two prophecies are not to be confused; then by a note of time, 'In those days, after that tribulation.' That is to say, the second End will happen after the first, but in the same Last Days; there is no indication of the length of the interval, one way or the other. And that is all the answer Jesus gives to the disciples' question, 'When shall these things be?' But he answers their second question, 'What shall be the sign when these things are about to be fulfilled?' explicitly. The signs of the End of the Temple were to be terrestrial—false teaching, famines, wars. But the signs of the End of Man will be celestial, cosmic. 'The sun shall be darkened, and the moon shall not give her light, and the stars shall be falling from heaven, and the powers that are in heaven shall be shaken. And *then* shall they see the Son of Man coming in clouds with power and great glory. And *then* shall he send forth the angels, and shall gather together his elect from the four winds, from the uttermost part of the earth to the uttermost part of heaven.' God will use the sky as his blackboard at the End, as he did at the first; and, when we see his writing there, we shall know that the End of earthly human history is near.

Leaving the matter of cosmic signs for the moment, let us go on to the last paragraph of the discourse. It is an exhortation to watch, to expect the End foretold, which to

37

its immediate hearers applied to both Ends, but for us, as for all since AD 71, refers only to the End of Man. In it Christ uses two analogies. The first is that of the fig-tree, whose bursting leaf-buds herald the approach of summer. The second is that of a man who, sojourning in another country, gives each of the servants in his *house*—notice the word—a task, but especially charges the porter to watch for his return, lest coming suddenly he find them sleeping. Thus the End appears paradoxically as both forewarned and sudden; the servants know their lord is coming, but do not know exactly when. In this paragraph, verse 30, occurs the statement, 'Verily, I say unto you, This generation shall not pass away, until all these things be fulfilled.'

'Verily,' *'amēn*, an adverb from the same root as *'emeth*, transliterated, not translated in the Greek, is the word with which our Lord was wont to preface his weightiest asseverations. 'I am telling you the truth', says the Truth. But, because of its apparent lack of truth, this statement has led many in the past to doubt the authenticity of the entire discourse. But wait a minute. As we have said, our Lord is dealing with two things, two Ends. A double vision in Isa. 7 was helped by the double meaning of a word; *ha-'almah* meant 'the young woman' for the first fulfilment, 'the virgin' for the second. Many words have double meaning, play on words is common in the Hebrew prophets, and the Word himself was no less subtle in his speech. There is an example in John 12.32. In Palestinian Aramaic it could have been taken either as 'I, if I be lifted up from the earth, will draw all men unto me', or as 'I, if I remove myself from Palestine . . .'; that is, 'if I go to the Gentiles.'[4] Greek in that case could not convey the *double entendre*, and the evangelist has given only the deeper reference to the uplifting on the cross. But the key word in Mark 13.30 has double meaning in both languages. Greek *genea* means 'race' or 'stock', as well as generation; and Hebrew–Aramaic *dôr* means generation, period or age, and habitation. 'Generation' meets the case for the first End, for the Temple was destroyed within the lifetime of our Lord's contemporaries. 'Race', 'age', and 'habitation' meet the second case, the End of Man. The human race, this Beth-El which is Man, shall not pass away till all these things be accomplished, nor shall this present Messianic Age.

St Matthew sets us another problem in his version of this same discourse; for in 24.29, which is parallel to Mark 13.24, he says, 'But *immediately*, after the tribulation of those days, the sun shall be darkened', etc. The word is *eutheōs*, a variant of *euthus*, of which St Mark is notoriously fond, though he does not use it here. There are two things that may be said about the First Evangelist. You can justify 'immediately' there, if you take it that the End of the Temple represents a pattern of tribulation, which is to be repeated all through these Last Days, until the End of Man is reached. Both evangelists speak of 'the *beginning* of the sufferings', which implies that the travail will continue until the final, fiercest pangs of the Last Day. The pattern is repetitive, undoubtedly; the only question is whether that repetition is included here. Otherwise, St Matthew's 'immediately' can only reflect the early Church's expectation of a speedy consummation, which some people find so upsetting. So let us look into the question of that hope.

It would have been surprising, had it not been cherished. The return of the Lord from death was so amazing to those so close to it in time, and the whole atmosphere of those post-Pentecostal days so full of the sense of his Presence, that it was natural for those who loved him to think of his visible Return as something that might happen any day—'wishful thinking', certainly, but surely better than our own indifference. All the same, there is much in the New Testament to suggest that, even from the first, the Church well knew that that Return might be delayed. When St Paul wrote 1 Thessalonians, in AD 51 or 52, he clearly expected to be among the living when the Lord returned; but in the second letter, very little later, he is emphatic that much must happen first. The implication of 'Why stand ye looking into heaven?' with which the heavenly messengers at the Ascension prefaced their promise of the Lord's Return,[5] was a blunt enjoinder to the Apostles to get on with their work on earth; which work the Lord himself had just defined as witnessing to him to the ends of the earth, hardly a task for a single generation. So in St Peter's sermon in Acts 3, vivid as is his hope of Christ's Return, he says expressly that the heavens must receive him, 'until the times of the restoration of all things'. And delay is stressed in our Lord's own parables. In that of the Ten Virgins, the Bridegroom tarries, and the virgins slumber and sleep, until at midnight they are suddenly aroused.[6] In that of the Pounds,[7] the servants have time to do much business while the nobleman their master is away in a far country, receiving for himself a kingdom; in the similar Parable of the Talents[8] the lord is absent for a long time. So also in the Parable of the Seed Growing Secretly,[9] which is believed by some people to be the original and authentic explanation of that of the Sower, there is a long process between sowing and harvest, and only 'when the fruit is ripe' does the farmer put in the sickle. The Parable of the Tares among the Wheat conveys the same idea. The analogy with the First Coming also would suggest delay. The early Church believed most firmly in the Lord's Return, and hoped that it would happen soon; that hope is probably reflected in St Matthew's Gospel. The Church today is pledged to the belief, and would do well to emulate the love that bred the hope.

Let us return to the question of the cosmic signs before the Second Coming. St Matthew's statement is the same as St Mark's, with the addition, after 'And the powers of heaven shall be shaken', of the following: '*And then shall appear the sign of the Son of Man in heaven, and then shall all the tribes of the earth mourn.*' St Luke makes a different addition. We will quote 21.25–8 in full. 'And there shall be signs in moon and stars; and upon the earth distress of nations, *in perplexity for the roaring of the sea and billows, men fainting for fear, and for expectation of the things which are coming on the world*, for the powers of heaven shall be shaken. And then shall they see the Son of Man coming in a cloud with power and great glory. *But when these things begin to come to pass, look up and lift up your heads; because your redemption draweth nigh.*'

St Luke speaks of 'redemption' in his Gospel twice; first in 2.38, where he says that the prophetess Anna, after seeing the infant Christ, 'spake of him to all them that looked for [the] redemption [*lutrōsis*] of Jerusalem'; and then here in 21.28, where he uses *apolutrōsis*, the same word strengthened with a prefix. The parallel between the two is obvious; but the verbs used are very different. The first is literally 'those that were looking forward to, expecting redemption', in a temporal sense; the pair in the second passage have reference to bodily position. The first is that already used in Luke 13.11 of the woman who 'was bowed together and could in no wise lift herself up', the other has 'your heads' expressly as its object. 'Straighten your backs and stand erect. *Sursum capita!* Look at the sky!'

We are considering this passage and its parallels as sober prophecies of what is some day going to happen. Because we believe in the Holy Spirit, we believe that the records of this great discourse are rooted in authentic apostolic memories of what the Lord Christ said that Tuesday evening as he sat with them, 'over against the Temple' on

41

the Mount of Olives; and that the discourse as we have it is substantially dominical and true. Our Lord, then, says that the signs preceding his Return will be of cosmic origin and seen in heaven. Some people interpret the words symbolically; but his prophecies of false teaching, wars, and famines as signs of the End of the Temple were fulfilled as literally as were those of his own Passion and Death. He did not always speak in riddles, and we must face at least the possibility that he meant here exactly what he says. The fact that cosmic signs appear in certain myths and in apocalyptic writings neither invalidates their mention here nor necessitates their figurative interpretation. For, as St Peter says in a passage already partly quoted, God 'spake of the Restoration of all things', which is to ensue from Christ's Return, 'by the mouth of all his holy prophets since the world began.'[10] There are weighty reasons for thinking that the Creation myth about Great Deep, which sets the pattern of Divine deliverance, repeated later in the Exodus and in the prophecies of Restoration to Jerusalem, contains a core of fossil history. World-wide traditions tell of great catastrophes, including portents in the sky, long periods of darkness, sudden climatic changes, and inundations on a scale unknown in history. In the equally widespread conception of world ages, it is these catastrophes that mark off age from age; and widespread also is the notion that the End of the world will be as the Beginning; *Endzeit* and *Urzeit* will match. It is difficult to dismiss all this mass of human tradition, which carries with it the idea of water as the hostile element, the enemy, so strange in any case, seeing that water is essential for life, and doubly strange in psalms from rocky Palestine, as pure invention or as borrowings by one race from another. And there is further a cluster of puzzling physical phenomena which are puzzling no longer on the hypothesis of some terrestrial catastrophe from cosmic causes sufficient to produce not only great up-heaval of earth's crust but also some disturbance in her movements. There is, for instance, the Great Rift, known to have been formed in human times; there are also the vast crustal dislocations in South America in which an advanced though ancient civilisation appears to have been involved. What caused those fearful fractures and up-heavals, and what did the people experience, in the way of tidal waves and so forth, who were there when they took place? What should result from the survivors' memories of such events, except exactly such traditions as in fact we find?

I put this forward soberly, as something worthy of con-sideration with an open mind. We know that earth is part of heaven, every way. It seems that, in the past, when Man was young, God may have given him some forcible re-minders of the fact, and so have laid with our ancestors, the few survivors of those terrible events, the first founda-tions of the revelation which culminated in the Incarnation of his Son. Further, St John says that because God so loved the *cosmos*, he sent his Son; and *cosmos* can mean 'universe' as well as 'world'. That Son's Return to earth to fetch the lost sheep home is something of importance to the universe. How should it not be heralded by heavenly signs?

'When shall these things be?' We have to ask the ques-tion, though we cannot answer it. There are no cosmic signs, as yet; so we can hardly echo Donne's, 'What if this present were the world's last night?' But the pattern of tribulation that precedes the End does seem to be intensi-fied in our own day. Wars there have always been; but not two world-wide wars within a generation, nor wars so ghastly in their weapons and effects. Famines have always been; but the threat of universal famine, because the earth's supplying power has been so exploited that it no longer meets the needs of its inhabitants, is new. False teaching, persecutions, antichrists also seem increasing. 'When the Son of Man comes, will he find faith on earth?'[11]

It looks as though the tempo of the pangs was quickening.

8

THE END OF MAN

THE End of Man is the purpose for which he was created;
and Christ's Return to earth is necessary for its final and
complete fulfilment. He himself assumed manhood's perfection—perfection in the sense of full development, as well
as in the sense of sinlessness—for the first time at the Transfiguration, in the sight of Peter, James, and John.[1] The
Greek says, 'He was *metamorphosed* before them,' he
changed his form. Metamorphosis, change of form at
different stages on the way to perfection, is common in the
natural world, the most familiar instance being that of
the creature which ends up as a butterfly, after being
successively an egg, a caterpillar, and a chrysalis. The
Transfiguration of Christ suggests that Man also is a meta-
morphic creature, and that properly he passes through
two preparatory stages only before reaching his full
development, the pre- and the post-natal. For the teaching
of the Bible is that death, for Man, is the result of sin;[2]
the state of being dead is a third stage, put in between the
second and the last, as a remedial penalty for sin. And the
fact that our Lord deliberately reverted to his mortal form
on the Mount, and went thence to Jerusalem to die in it,
demonstrates the truth of his own saying, 'No man taketh
my life from me, I lay it down of myself. I have power to
lay it down, and I have power to take it again.'[3] For after
death he passed again to his perfection, this time finally. In
that perfected body, that yet bore the marks of what its
larval form had borne on Calvary, he was touched and

45

handled, as well as seen and heard, by many of his friends during the forty days. All that we know of Manhood perfected, Man in his final form, that perfect form that God intends us all to reach, all that St Paul, for instance, teaches about the risen body and its relation to the former earthly one,[4] is based on their direct, first-hand experience of the Risen Lord in AD 29.

Thus he, the New and sinless Adam, completed Man's predestined course by the fallen Adam's road; he brought our manhood to perfection by the four-stage process, not the three. In so doing, he reversed the Fall, effected Atonement, and opened the way, his way, the Way that he is, for Man as a whole to follow and by it to come to the Father. It follows that Man, as well as individual men, must die. The End of Man, in the positive, purposive sense, involves the End of larval Man in the conclusive sense.

The immediate purpose of the Second Coming in the Creeds is Judgement. 'He shall come again in glory to judge both the quick and the dead.' 'The Resurrection of the dead and the Life of the World (or Age) to Come', or, as the Apostles' Creed puts it, 'the Resurrection of the Body and the Life Everlasting', come not in the middle section about God the Son but at the end of the third, as the final work of God the Holy Spirit, the Lord and the Life-Giver. Nevertheless, it is the plain teaching of Scripture that the Resurrection of Man will precede the Judgement; as the *Quicunque* puts it, 'At whose [that is, Christ's] Coming all men shall rise again with their bodies and shall give account for their own works.' They will be judged in the final body for what they made of themselves, or let God make of them, in the earthly one. Thus the four things, the Second Coming, the Resurrection, the Judgement, and the Everlasting Life, all hang together; you cannot have any one of them without the other three.

46

The scriptural passages about this great Finale are full of paradox; and how indeed should it be otherwise, since paradox is contradiction, yet completion, and the thing here envisaged is the final perfecting of all that is? The very words used of the Coming are paradoxical; for the two nouns *parousia* and *epiphaneia* mean presence and manifestation;[5] only the verbs, such as the 'shall come' of Acts 1.11 and the 'shall descend' of 1 Thess. 4.16, give the idea of a Return to earth, as though he were not all the time on earth already. But there is no confusion; for the paradox is rooted in the experience of the forty days. He did not 'come' to the Apostles in the upper room; he just was there. Nor, even after they had 'seen him go', could the Presence thus revealed be doubted when it was not visible.

The language about the resurrection of believers also is paradoxical. Those who are in Christ already share his risen life, yet look to be raised hereafter. But here again there is no real confusion; the paradox of the mystical and literal resurrections is only that of the *Tetélestai* itself, the potential Consummation and the actual. And, whatever else may be obscure, it is quite clear that the Resurrection will be general. *Man* will rise, Man as an entity, the human *genea* complete will be brought by Christ at his Second Coming to its final form; and in—perhaps we might say *by*—that form it will be judged. 'This is the will of him that sent me', says our Lord in John 6.39, 'that of *all that* which he hath given me I should lose nothing, but should raise it up at the Last Day'. The general neuter, *pān*, the whole thing, is contrasted with the specific masculine *pās* in the next verse, where the resurrection of believers only is in view. 'For this is the will of my Father, that *every one* that beholdeth the Son and believeth on him should have eternal life, and I will raise *him* up at the Last Day.'

After the Resurrection, Judgement. Here the same

paradox obtains; for Judgement, like the Kingdom of God and the resurrection of believers, appears in the New Testament as present as well as future. But the relation of the two is clear. The final Judgement will reveal the results of the process of judgement, of sifting and sorting, which Christ initiated when he came into the world, and will conclude it. What do the Scriptures tell us of that august, supreme event?

First, that the holy angels will accompany the Judge.[6] The ninety and nine will be with the Shepherd when he comes to bring the lost sheep home and so complete their number. The host of heaven, whom a few men saw the night that Christ was born, will be seen by all men when he comes again. They watch our conflict now,[7] though we have little sense of them. What will it be at the Judgement, to be aware of them, as well as of all Man, and also to see Christ?

The second thing that emerges is that the Judgement of Man will be the judgement of individual men; and the criterion each man's personal reaction to and treatment of the Person of the Judge. Our Lord's own teaching puts this in two ways. There is the conscious, direct encounter, as in the passage quoted above; beholding him challenges to faith in him, which surely is to love him. There is also the indirect encounter with the Christ in other men, as set forth in the tremendous picture of the separation of the sheep and goats.[8] Both come to the same thing. It is love that matters; and on love and by love's Self, who bears our nature and has travelled by our road, will Man, and men, be judged in the revealing light of the Last Day.

God gave free-will to Man, because only a person, a being with free-will, is capable of love. But freedom pulls both ways; if you can love, you can refuse to love. Under no circumstances will God remove free-will from Man; for to do so would be to go back on his creation and make him less than Man. There is therefore the awful possibility—and we must face it squarely—that some men, even at the last when Love Incarnate meets them face to face, may spurn his love and still refuse belief. Some, and among them the great Origen, one of the deepest thinkers and most passionate lovers of our Lord the Church has ever known, have seen in the final and absolute separation of the goats from the sheep and the tares from the wheat a solemn warning of what may be, rather than a prophecy of what will certainly occur; they have at least dared to hope that, in the end, the love of God in Christ will break down all barriers and save the human race in its entirety. Whether this universal view is justified, we shall not know until the Last Day comes. Till then, the warning stands.

The *Last* Day. The last of these Last Days in which we are now living, the End of mortal Man's terrestrial history. For those who love, what follows in 'the Life of the Age to Come'?

'Eye hath not seen', says St Paul, with reminiscence of the Third Isaiah, 'nor ear heard, neither have entered into the heart of man, what things God hath prepared for them that love him.'[9]

Let us go back to the Apocalypse, with a quotation from which this book began, remembering that a special blessing rests upon its readers, remembering also that 'they understand but little who understand only what can be explained'.[10] Elsewhere in the Bible we look up to heaven from earth; in the Apocalypse we look at earth, and the Church on earth, the Bride and Body of Christ, as they appear from heaven. We are shown the Church in the throes of the great tribulation, in her passion and death and in her resurrection. We see her very judgement as taking place in heaven. Then comes a surprise. She should ascend to heaven, according to the pattern; the Son of Man should bear her to the Father's throne. Instead, the

Bride herself comes down from heaven to earth; and earth, as well as heaven, is made new.[11] It seems when evil is no more, there will no longer be any up or down. In the same chapter we are shown the Church, Mankind redeemed in Christ, as New Jerusalem; and here again is a surprise. There is no Temple in her; and the reason given is not that now the City is all Temple, all Beth-El, though that no doubt is true; but that the Lord God the Almighty and the Lamb are the Temple thereof. God, Man's In-dweller, is now indwelt by Man.

'He who testifies to these things says, "Surely I am coming soon! Amen. Come, Lord Jesus!"'

9

THE PRACTICE OF
EXPECTATION

OUR Lord has laid on us all the command to watch for his Coming.[1] Expectation is a Christian duty, never more urgent than at the present day, and never more neglected. For this is a dark hour, even if not yet that darkest that must come before the Dawn; and, if we are to keep our faith and sanity, we must face it for what it is, the filling up of the Passion of Christ in his mystical Body, that must precede the final Resurrection, as travail precedes birth. It may be that our lack of faith delays the Consummation, as Israel's lack of faith delayed her coming home to Canaan. How can we quicken our faith in the Last Things and practise expectation? Here are a few suggestions that may help.

We must, of course, pray specifically for a lively, integrated faith, because faith is the gift of God alone. But we can help ourselves by finding pegs, if one may use the term, to hang it on. The act of turning eastward for the Creed is meant to be such a peg, a conscious and deliberate act of looking for the Dawn. The Holy Eucharist is the perpetual memorial of the death of Christ until his coming again; there is the supreme focus for deliberate faith. 'O God, make speed . . .,' 'O Lord, make haste . . .,' so many times repeated, are vessels we can fill with expectation; and the Angelus collect, in which we pray that by Christ's Cross and Passion we may be brought to the glory of his Resurrection, is another. And, in an individual context, 'before the whole company of heaven' in the *Confiteor* may well remind the penitent that they will be his audience at the Last Judgement too.

Next, and most obviously, we must read and read again the passages of Scripture that bear on the Last Things, pondering and chewing them in loving faith and hope, as Simeon, that prince of watchful porters, must have chewed on passages like that in Malachi, which later was fulfilled before his eyes.[2] If a few people get together over this, they help each other. The references in this book are given in the hope that here and there a study group may find them useful. They are far from exhaustive, of course, but should serve for a start.

Thirdly, there is the Christian Year. Once you begin to see things whole, there is hardly any point in it at which the Consummation of all things does not come into view. From Christmas to Ascension we follow our Lord's life, each stage of which both has and is to have its saving counterpart in Man's experience; and at Whitsun we think of the Life of the World to Come as the ultimate work of the life-giving Spirit. Of separate feasts, that of the Dedication centres on the New Jerusalem, the City and the Bride of God; that of Christ the King (if we keep it) centres on him as he now is in heaven and as he thence shall come; and the Second Sunday after Easter reminds us that Man is the lost sheep whom the Good Shepherd came from heaven to save and to reunite at last, in heaven, with the flock. And so on. And also there is Advent. What of that?

Someone has said that, in the Advent liturgy, the First and Second Comings struggle like Jacob and Esau as to which shall be first born, and Christmas wins. In most of our thinking and teaching Christmas not only wins but holds the field almost alone, an only child, despite the liturgy. Several causes have contributed to this lopsidedness of faith. The humble Coming in the past is on our level and can be visualised; the glorious future one defeats imagination; indeed, the medieval efforts to depict it repel the modern mind as much as Christmas cribs and plays attract it. Moreover, cranks have vainly prophesied the End of the World for some particular date so often, that we have come to doubt if it will ever end. The only 'last thing' most of us look forward to is death; and we are much too busy before Christmas to think much of that.

God forbid that we should think in Advent less of the Nativity or prepare less carefully for Christmas sacraments. It is our Christian duty so to do—but only half of it. We must go on to see our Lord's two Comings in their relation to each other and to that single Coming to the Father which they serve; we must prepare to meet him not only at the altar, but when he comes again. That Second Coming is not foretold in the New Testament alone; some of the Old Testament prophecies (as well as the types) look forward to the Consummation too. The vision in Isa. 52 is one of these; and we look for another sudden coming of the Lord whom we seek to his Temple, in the figurative sense, besides the lowly literal one that Simeon saw. Some people may find such passages as these the easiest approach. But, be this as it may, it is for pastors and teachers to lead the way and seize the Advent opportunity, this very year, to teach the Creed in its integrity, boldly and without apology. If they do so, the flocks will follow them; and the effort of teaching the Last Things will quicken their own faith and longing for our Lord's Return. 'Behold, I stand at the door and knock,' he says.[3] He waits for us to want him and to say, 'Come in!'

Besides the foregoing helps to the practice of Christian expectation, there are visual aids. People will differ in what strikes them here. But every butterfly is a reminder that 'it does not yet appear what we shall be'; and then there is the sky. It is recorded of St Ignatius Loyola that, from the time of his conversion, he was an inveterate star-gazer; and it is always good for us to look away from ourselves and the present and earth in general, and from our normal preoccupation with means rather than ends, to that immensity of mystery whence he shall come, and where the sign of the Son of Man shall one day herald his Coming. And one particular constellation seems a sort of picture of the subject of this book. There is One Coming of Christ, the One Man, to the Father in heaven, and in the process of that coming there are the three great moments of From, Into, and Thence, the last of which will lead to the Consummation. That is the way in which God fulfils the purpose of Creation and puts right the wrong, by making evil minister its own defeat. Cassiopeia[4] is like a W, the first limb down, the second up, the third one down again. The fourth and last also goes up, and there it stays.

'And all this showed he full blissfully', wrote Julian of Norwich in 1373, 'signifying thus:

> *See! I am God: see! I am in all thing;*
> *see! I do all thing;*
> *see! I lift never My hands off My works,*
>   *nor ever shall without end;*
> *see! I lead all thing to the end I ordained it to*
>   *from without beginning,*
> *by the same Might, Wisdom and Love*
>   *whereby I made it.*
> *How should anything be amiss?"*

PART II

INTRODUCTION

IN THE Christian revelation there is one Coming, and that a Coming to Heaven, and there is one Man who comes. Those were the themes, derived from Dan. 7, propounded in Part I. As the first of those, the single Coming, was chiefly dealt with there, our aim now is to amplify the other, the theme of the one Man, by trying to unpack a little of the meaning latent in two chapters of St Paul's Epistles, and more particularly in the following statements:

The first Man, Adam, became a living being; the last Adam became a life-giving spirit.

The first Man was from the earth, a man of dust; the second Man is from heaven.

As in Adam all die, so also in Christ shall all be made alive.   (1 Cor. 15.45, 47 and 22—RSV)

His gifts were that some should be apostles, some prophets, some evangelists, some pastors and teachers, for the equipment of the saints, for the work of ministry, for the building up of the Body of Christ, until we all attain to the unity of the faith and of the knowledge of the Son of God, to mature manhood, to the measure of the stature of the fulness of Christ.

(Eph. 4.11–13—RSV)

Put another way, the theme of this second part is that Man and the Church are meant by God to be the same: they were so at the first, and he is working now, both through the Church as we know it, and beyond the Church in ways we do not know, to make them so again.

57

10

THE MEANING OF 'CHURCH'

HAVING thus specified our subject, we must now consider what the word 'Church' means. Words are like stones on the seashore; being for ever battered on the lips of men, they get worn down, and sometimes their original shape gets changed so much that their basic meaning gets obscured. 'Church' is a case in point. It started as the Greek word *kyriakon*, a neuter adjective used as a noun and meaning the Lord's own, and specially his house. This radical meaning of Church is obviously wholly apt for that for which we use it; for the Body of Christ figures in Scripture also as his holy house or palace-temple, wherein it pleaseth him to dwell.[1]

But *kyriakon* is never used for Church in the New Testament; the word there is *ekklēsia*. The literal meaning of *ekklēsia* is that-which-is-called-out, and in ordinary Greek it denoted originally the legislative assembly that was called out to its meetings by a crier; which calling out, we may observe, was twofold and of corporate intent: members were called out both from among non-members and also from wherever they happened to be to go to the place of assembly, and the purpose of their calling was that they might serve the interests of the state, the common good. Three centuries before New Testament times, however, the word *ekklēsia* had been appropriated by the translators of the Septuagint, the Greek Old Testament, as one of two renderings for the Hebrew word *qāhāl*, which means there the assembly or congregation of Israel, God's Chosen People, and so denoted that People as a whole. The alternative term was *synagōgē*, which was an exact match for *qāhāl* in its literal meaning; and in point of fact you find *synagōgē* rendering *qāhāl* in the first four books of the Pentateuch, and again in the prophets, but in Deuteronomy, with one exception, and from there onwards to the end of the historical books you find *ekklēsia*. But by the first century AD the two words were no longer interchangeable; for *synagōgē* had come to be the accepted term for the Jewish people as the Greek world knew them, meeting for non-sacrificial worship in their synagogues in every place.

The New Testament writers, therefore, were left without a choice; only *ekklēsia* remained to denote God's new Chosen People, the Church of Pentecost, and to distinguish it from that from which it sprang.

To sum up. From the original meanings of two Greek words for Church we have got five ideas:

From *kyriakon*: (i) that it is, in general, the Lord's own possession, and
(ii) in particular, his house;
From *ekklēsia*: (iii) that it is a people (and consists of persons) called out from others who are not so called, and
(iv) called out also from one place to another;
(v) that the body thus called out comes out to serve the good of the whole body of which it is a part.

All those ideas are covered by any word for Church in use today. The actual English word, for instance, comes from *kyriakon* but includes the three *ekklēsia* ideas; while words like French *église*, that come from *ekklēsia*, cover the sense of *kyriakon* too. The five ideas belong together; and when we say in the Creed, 'I believe in the Holy Catholic Church', we might perhaps call some of them to mind.

59

THE GENESIS CREATION
NARRATIVES

PEOPLE nowadays are wont to apologise for the account of
human origins in Genesis; we know now—so they tell us—
that it is 'not historical'. Just what they mean by that is not
explained. But this at least is certain: if Man, the human
race to which we all belong, in point of fact was *not*
created in God's Image, very good, and if he did *not* subse-
quently fall from his first estate by his own act, then the
rest of the Bible is meaningless. If there was no first Adam,
what sense is there in calling Christ the Second? Apart
from Man's transgression, what need was there of repara-
tion, atonement and redemption? And how could the
Image of God be restored in Man, if it was never given?

It cannot be stated too strongly that the only apology
owing in regard to these chapters in Genesis is to God the
Holy Spirit, their ultimate Author, from those who doubt
their value. After all, he was there when Man began. He
knows what happened; and he also knows the best way to
communicate to us the things we need to know and have
the power to grasp about those two exceedingly remote
events that set the course for human history. If we believe
in the Holy Spirit, as we say in the Creed that we do, we
must trust him for that.

We must trust him, and at the same time face another
fact. The divine Scriptures, as the Fathers loved to call
them, are human writings too. The Holy Spirit is, as we
said, their ultimate author; it is his single authorship

that makes the Bible one. But he did not send it down from heaven ready-made; for that is not the way in which God works. It comes to us, from him and full of him, by way of countless free-willed human agents, employed by him for ends beyond their ken. These opening chapters in particular are the fruit of an age-long process of transmission, oral for unnumbered centuries before a word was written, but guided by him patiently and surely to its appointed end, their present form. Hoary and venerable as they are, we have no right nor reason to expect them to be easy; we shall have to wrestle with them —as indeed with all the Holy Bible—much as we wrestle with the stubborn earth to get our food from it.

Bearing that paradox in mind, let us get humbly now to our inquiry. First, it is obvious that Gen. 1 and 2 contain two narratives. Although in our translations the point of junction is obscured, there is quite clearly one that speaks of God (*'Elōhîm*) and one that speaks of the Lord God (*Yahweh 'Elōhîm*). Neither of these describes Creation absolute; in both the earth in some sense is already there when the creative work begins. In the 'God' story, a chaos of waters covers the earth and all is dark; over Deep, however, there broods the Spirit of God. Then God says 'Let there be light!', and there is light; and that is the first of six 'days' or stages, by which at God's word the primaeval chaos gives place to the orderly earth we know. The firmament—that is, the sky—is created on the second day; then the dry land and vegetation; then the luminaries, sun, moon, and stars; then fishes and birds; then the land animals and, after them but still on the sixth 'day', Man, *'ādām*,[1] made by God in his own image and in both sexes. This Man, already in the plural number, is bidden to be fruitful and multiply, to replenish and subdue the earth, and to have dominion over all living creatures on the earth. The vegetation of the earth is given for food for Man

61

and beast alike. Then follows the blesséd, holy, seventh 'day', when God rests from his work of creation; and the story ends in the first part of the fourth verse of Gen. 2 with the words: 'These are the generations of the heaven and of the earth, when they were created.'

The 'Lord God' Creation story now takes over. The Revised Version is easier to follow here than the Authorised; having put a full stop after 'created' in verse 4 to mark the end of the 'God' story, you have only to begin the next word, 'In', with a capital, and delete the 'and' at the beginning of verse 5. You then get this:

> In the day that the Lord God made earth and heaven, no plant of the field was yet in the earth . . . and there was no *'ādām* to till the ground.

The sequence of events is then as follows. The Lord God forms the *'ādām* [out of] dust from the ground (*'ādamāh*) and breathes into his nostrils the breath of life; thus the *'ādām* becomes a *nephesh ḥayyah*, that is, a living soul. He then plants a garden eastwards, in Eden, with trees and a four-fold river, and puts the new-made *'ādām* into it, to dress it and to till it, and with freedom to eat of all the trees save one. Thus far the *'ādām* is alone. But now the Lord God says, 'It is not good for the *'ādām* to be alone; I will make a help to correspond to him.' The next two verses (2.19 f.) are plainly a parenthesis; they relate that the Lord God had (previously) formed all the animals and brought them to the *'ādām* to name, but among them no such answering help was found. The thread of verse 18 is picked up in verse 21; the Lord God acts on his resolution and forms the help required from one of the *'ādām*'s own ribs while he is in deep sleep, and presents her to him, just as he had presented the animals before. The *'ādām* says on seeing her: 'This is now bone of my bones and flesh of my flesh; she shall be called woman (*'ishshah*) because she was taken out of man (not '*ādām*, Man as distinct from the beasts, but '*ish*, the male). 'Therefore', says verse 24, a later comment on the ancient story probably, '*therefore shall a man leave his father and his mother, and shall cleave unto his wife, and they shall be one flesh*'. The Creation story ends with the statement that 'they were both naked, the '*ādām* and his '*ishshah*, and were not ashamed'.

That is the substance of the narratives. The Hebrew words are given to point the fact that in both of them '*ādām* is a generic, not a proper name. '*The* Man'—it nearly always has the article—is such, as distinct from and superior to the animals. The significance of these accounts will be best treated in a separate chapter. Before we go to it, however, let us put forward a suggestion which may ease the subject, at any rate for some.

On the evidence of the fossils found in the stratified rocks, geologists divide the pre-human history of life on this planet into ages or periods, all of immense duration. The earliest, Cuvier and his school, observing that the dominant type of life appeared to change abruptly from one main period to the next, concluded that each ended with a great catastrophe that killed off all existing forms of life, after which God created a new one, so to speak from scratch. D'Orbigny, one of Cuvier's pupils, made out a case for twenty-seven creations! This theory held the field until Darwin, observing that, for all these startling changes in predominance, the fossils showed an ordered sequence from lower forms to higher, put out the theory of evolution. For a long time after that it was believed that evolution explained everything, and the catastrophic theory was relegated to the rubbish-heap. But now it seems we were a bit too hasty. There is no doubt about evolution; every living organism starts individually from a single cell; and it seems quite certain that all life has developed from unicellular forms. But that does not explain why—to take but one example—the great reptiles that flourished in the Jurassic and Cretaceous periods disappeared at the end of the latter almost entirely, leaving the little mammals, which before were hardly beginning, to take their place as the dominant fauna of the ensuing age. Only one thing, apparently, could account for such phenomena as that—namely, a relatively sudden and drastic change of climate and environment fatal to type A in every case, but favourable to the previously incipient and struggling B, which from the very struggle had developed a greater power to adapt itself to change. And—again apparently—it seems that the only thing that could effect such change on earth would be a modification of one or more of its movements, a change in the tilt of its axis to the plane of its orbit, and/or in the length of the orbit itself and so in its position with relation to the sun; which change could be effected only by a cosmic cause.

So much for pre-human times. But all the world over there are myths of world ages, similarly marked off by catastrophes, *in human times*. The details vary; but signs in heaven, along with floods and seismic disturbances on a scale unknown in what is commonly described as history, are prominent. There is frequent mention also of great fires that destroyed all vegetation and almost all mankind, and of darkness that lasted several generations. Myths often have a core of fossil history, and it is difficult to believe that such as these could have taken shape without some factual basis. Moreover, belief in world ages is implicit in the New Testament teaching that the Last Age, 'these last days', began with Christ's first Coming and will end with his Return; and he himself taught that that great consummation will be heralded by cosmic signs. The same belief lies behind the phrase 'unto the ages of ages' to denote eternity; and our familiar form of it, 'world without end', means just the same, for 'world' is *wer-alt*, man-age or period of human history.² As Christians, we would seem to be committed to world ages, and to the prospect of a catastrophic ending for the last, at any rate. Why should we doubt it? There is something essentially authentic in the thought of those long peaceful periods, human and pre-human, divided from each other by relatively short times of stress, from each of which a straitened but enduring remnant emerges to a roomy place and a higher mode of life. The God we know is working there, on a principle we know. St Irenaeus, developing a thought that St Justin Martyr derived from a passage in Plato, says that the Son of God is crucified in the whole universe, being inscribed in the form of the Greek letter *Chi*—that is, a saltire or St Andrew's cross—upon it all.³

Now let us return to Genesis and see what we can make of the 'God' story of Creation on the hypothesis that it is grounded, no matter how remotely, on the survivors' memories of some great cataclysm, perhaps the one that saw the making of the Rift, the crustal fracture of which the Jordan valley forms the northern end. It begins with water and darkness, for that is all these few poor humans can remember. Then comes the marvel of light, seen for the first time; then, as the volcanic dust and vapours clear still more, and water-masses settle into their new beds, the sky appears, followed by dry land on which plant life soon regains a footing, and finally the sun and moon and stars. Animal life, slower to reproduce itself than vegetable, begins to re-establish itself in noticeable quantity next; and lastly Man himself, whose reproduction rate is slower than that of most animals, begins to multiply and to re-people the new surface of the earth.

This sequence of events thus makes good sense for a period of settling down after a great terrestrial disturbance. But how can the creation of Man himself be fitted into a

65

frame that postulates men's own dim memory of what occurred? Here again we offer a suggestion, which readers can take or leave. We know that the prophets sometimes saw two future things as one; Isaiah, for instance, foretold that a young woman then living would shortly bear a child, and at the same time prophesied that Christ would be born of a virgin, which did not come to pass for centuries. So our suggestion for easing the problem here is that in the Creation narratives two *past* events are superimposed and so appear as one, and were indeed believed to be one by the people who told the stories. Of the re-establishment of Man on earth after his almost entire extermination in the last catastrophe there were dim traditions of incalculable age. Of the even remoter event of Man's original creation there could be no tradition; for, even if God gave him knowledge of it, his language, newborn with himself as we shall shortly see, could not have been sufficient to pass the knowledge on. But the Creator knew both how he made mankind and what mankind needed to know about itself. So into the human tradition of what took place much later he breathed that necessary measure of the truth about what happened at the first. And that inspired content must we now consider.

THE FIRST MAN

THE two Creation narratives are complementary to each other, and in this chapter we shall treat them as a unity.

The creation of the *'ādām*, Man, is plainly represented as the peak point of the creative process, and as a direct and special act of God. At God's word the earth brought forth vegetation of itself; the water and the earth in the same way brought forth the animals. But God said, '*Let us make* Man', and formed him directly, as a potter forms a vessel on his wheel; he himself inbreathed him with the breath of life that made him *nephesh ḥayyah*. St Luke, tracing our Lord's descent from the first Man, sums up this uniqueness by saying that Adam was a son of God. And of our Lord's own origin he tells us that he was conceived and born by a human mother alone, through the overshadowing power of the Holy Spirit.[1] That is to say, the Second Adam also came into being by a direct new-creative act of God, an intervention by him in the normal process of his own creation. Thus the Holy Thing that was born of Mary was at once an integral part of all prevenient manhood and indeed all life, *and* something wholly new; in the Divine Humanity Man began again.

The two Men, therefore, are represented in the Bible as being alike in their beginnings, as well as in their later course, in which the Second takes the First one's road, apart from sin, in order to redeem him.[2] How, in the light of modern knowledge, are we to understand the former new creation? I put the following forward as a reverent conjecture. Our divine Lord had ancestors, but they were only men. Adam had ancestors, but they were less than men. In order to make Man, must not the Holy Spirit have overshadowed a sub-human mother, who was the fruit and peak of the age-long process of evolution that he himself had guided to that very end?

But whatever the manner of the new creation, 'the Adam' was certainly the first of his kind and—at the outset—all there was of it. And the nature of his uniqueness is conveyed in Genesis by the statement that God created him after his own image, to resemble him. We may see that likeness in two ways. He was like God from the first in that he was a rational, free-willed and moral being; he was like God thereafter in that he was made to be not only an individual rational being, but also a social and creative one, thus reflecting in himself the One-in-Manyness of God the Trinity. Let us consider first his rationality.

The Greek word for rational is *logikos*, and its opposite is *alogos*. The fundamental meaning of the former is 'having speech', and of the latter 'speechless' or 'lacking speech'. The Lord God brought the animals to Adam to see what he would call them; when the Man's unaccustomed lips formed names for them, then human speech was born. And when the Lord God put him in the garden, 'to dress it and to till it', he set his feet on another distinctively human path; for he would have to fashion tools for gardening, and animals do not do that.

But there was more than that to Adam's rationality, incipient though it was. The central point, the crowning wonder was that he *knew* what God would have him do. That knowledge cannot at that stage have clothed itself in words; it must have been intuitive, and the Man's response in the same way the wordless prayer of love. It is interesting to reflect that prayer must have preceded saying prayers, as always it transcends it.

The world was literally his in those first days of Man's humanity; for the Lord God had given him dominion over every living thing. But he was lonely; for the irrational animals, for all their beauty and their close relationship, could not provide an answering help for him. And so God made the *woman*, so called because he formed her from the man.

The creation of the woman is a very great mystery, and cannot be explained in terms of any knowledge that we have today. It seems as though the language must be figurative; if that is so, then we can be certain that this particular figure is the nearest we can get to understanding this fundamental truth about the relation between man and woman; for otherwise the Holy Spirit would not have given us the story in this form. And the priority of the man, and the manner of the woman's derivation from him are of very great significance, as we shall see later.

Another point is this. The first Creation story does not mention Eve; it simply says, 'And God created Man in his own image, in the image of God created he *him*; male and female created he *them*.' The implication is that the image of God in Man consists in the male-and-femaleness, the fact of sex, in the human race as a whole. And you get light on that from what the second narrative says about the creation of the woman after and from the man. Male and female are not the same as masculine and feminine; sex is not the same as gender; but only its particular expression in organic life. Gender in creation is an inclusive reality; other created things besides plants and animals and men have qualities of masculinity or the reverse, although they have not sex.[3] But the ultimate reality of gender transcends the created order, for it lies in the relation between God himself and all that he has made. He is the Masculine, creation is the corresponding feminine.

Put in another way, that means that he is the Lover, the

Husband, the Possessor, and creation is the object of his love. But love is in its essence mutual, as in the Blessed Trinity; and that is why creation culminates in rational Man, who only of all earthly creatures has the power both to know himself beloved by God and to return his love. And Man himself reflects this mystery of love between God and the created order made conscious in himself, both in that he includes both male and female, and in that the being of the latter is secondary and derived.

Here, then, is the ground of the unique holiness of Christian marriage; here is the reason why that relationship takes precedence of every other, even the sacred bond that binds a son to his parents. Here, too, is the ultimate source of the conception of the Lord as Husband of his People,[4] of the interpretation, Jewish as well as Christian, of the Song of Songs on the same lines, and of the crowning vision of the Apocalypse, the Marriage of the Lamb.[5] Adam-and-Eve were Man, humanity; and Man was *kyriakon*, the Lord's own, the Bride-elect of God, his chosen creature, his *ekklēsia*, his Church. As such, he was the link —not missing, but in place—between God and the whole created order.

We cannot date these days of innocence, nor yet locate the spot on earth where they were spent. But they took place in time and space, they happened; God knows their where and when, though we do not, and the sun and the moon and the stars that we see today looked down upon them too. And we ourselves were there, for we were *in* our father Adam when he lived.

That is a difficult thought for our individualistic and hypercivilised age; but the fact remains. All Man was in The Man at the beginning, just as the ultimate tree is in the acorn whence by slow degrees it grows. If we could look down on the earth and watch the increase of our race from the beginning, we should see it as a single organism, spreading outwards from its single origin to cover the whole earth, like a living lava-flow. There is only one Man, as we have emphasised before. Men—human beings—are small but integral parts of Man, just as the individual living cells that make your body are small but integral parts of you. Therefore the individual makes no sense alone; all his significance is relative. And God is the God of the living, not of the dead. All who have ever been, although we call them dead, are still alive in him, waiting —as we await—the consummation of his purpose for the race.

I have dwelt on this at some length, because it is exceedingly important. Origen interpreted the Socratic precept, 'Know thyself', as meaning for the Christian, in effect: 'Know your own dignity and worth, know yourself created in God's image, the object of his love; and only then go on to recognise how much that image is defaced in you and so co-operate with God in getting it restored.' St Bernard taught the same; it is indeed the only rational course thus to take *all* the facts about ourselves into account. Let us lay hold with all our might of the great fact: we lived in Adam in his potential perfection, before his fall involved us in his death.

Just one more subject calls for notice before we bring this chapter to a close. We have spoken of Adam as being at once the culmination of all previous life, and the rational link between God and the rest of his creation. That is a truth that looks two ways. On its Godward side it invests Man's rationality with a nobler meaning than that of the ability to speak, divine and aweful as that power is. The Man as created is *logikos* in the further sense that he is the proper home of the *Logos*, the Word of God by whom all things were made, the only earthly creature able to open its door to him of its own will. On the creatureward side of this same truth two things stand out. The first is that, until the Fall, there was no barrier in that direction either; Man was as close to the animals, from whose irrational ranks he had so newly come, as he was to God, and he was knit to them by a like wordless bond of understanding love. The second striking thing—and this holds good even for fallen Man—is that you simply cannot say where his connection with creation stops. It does not stop at the frontier of organic life; for he is the Earthborn, the *'ādām* from the *'adāmāh* and the body with which his mind and spirit are so mysteriously linked is made of the same elements as are the sun and moon and stars, lives by the power of the sun, and is a constant thoroughfare for cosmic rays. There is no escaping the fact that Man is a cosmic creature; is he God's instrument—or, rather, agent—for the redemption of the universe, into which evil had already come before his time? Is God's choice of this small planet, out of the celestial myriads, for the home of Man the first example of his choosing the weak things of the cosmos to confound the mighty, the prelude to his choice of little Palestine, out of all earthly countries, for the homeland of his Chosen People and the scene of the Incarnate Life?

There are suggestions in the Bible that this may be so. But we anticipate. We know only too well that now, of all God's creatures, Man himself stands in most need of cleansing and redemption. In the next chapter we must think how that immeasurable tragedy befell.

13

THE FALL OF MAN

THE story of the Fall of Man in Gen. 3 is the continuation of the 'Lord God' story of Creation in the latter part of chapter 2, and stands in very close relation to it.

We have seen that rational Man was the link between God and Creation. We have also noted that throughout the history of life every advance on the physical plane issued from difficulties overcome; living forms progressed, not when conditions were easy, but when something *crossed* them, and they had to fight. This divine principle required that Man, inchoate creature that he was in spirit as in body, must be thus tested on the higher, as well as on the lower plane, in order to attain his full development.

Difficulty is not evil in itself; one of the most authentic joys in life is getting over fences. But according to this story there was evil in the world before Man and along with him, before it got inside him. No word is said about its origin; it is just there, expressed in animal form, but none the less the personal Enemy, seeking to spoil God's work and thwart his plan. Man, in the persons of the first man and his woman, have been told not to do a certain thing. They know what disobedience will entail; if they transgress God's bidding, they will die. The Enemy's attack is directed against their faith in God's dependability, his truth, and so against their love. 'Yea, hath God said . . . ?' The implication is, 'Well, and what if he has? He only said it because he knows that, if you do it, you will be as gods yourselves, knowing good and evil!'

As gods—they who already were made in the image of God, and had it in them to develop in his likeness! The temptation is to take the easy way, to reach the goal at once without the uphill climb. It is no accident that this inspired story centres on a tree; for a tree with its straight trunk and horizontal branches is a cross, and it is the principle of the cross that the Enemy is here inciting the woman to evade. He lies to her; there is no upward road except through testing. If Man had stood the test, and gone on standing it, he would have grown. But he did not.

When the temptation overcame the Man, in both his parts, the female and the male, the link between God and his world, so long and lovingly prepared, fell out of place. Man was no longer *kyriakon*, the Lord's Own, the Church, when once he had rebelled.

'O thou Adam, what hast thou done? For though it was thou that sinned, the evil is not fallen upon thee alone, but upon all of us that come of thee.'[1]

That is the natural reaction of the sons of Adam, in view of the result of his transgression for themselves. We were in Adam when he sinned, and so in him we die; we inherit from him a lamed and vitiated nature, and live on a planet cursed for his sake. But the Lord God was far more wronged than we. He was wronged utterly, and Man—in whom we were—was utterly at fault. And Man had been so beautiful. How could God bear to see his work thus spoiled, his purpose thwarted? Yet, being God, and good, he could not give it up; neither could he remit the law that death must follow on Man's sin. What then was God to do?

That is the divine dilemma as St Athanasius saw it.[2] But before we can answer the question, we must consider the significance of human death.

The difference between Man as God made him and

even the highest of the animals, though slight in many ways, was in the most important *all* the difference. In rationality he had the thing that turned the scale, and made the spiritual side of him preponderate. It ruled the physical in him, as he himself ruled all the lower creatures. They die, because in them the balance is reversed; the physical outweighs the higher element, and death results when the span of their life is completed. For them it is natural; for Man it is not. If he had kept the balance of his nature, he would not have died.

But Man, when in this primal state of honour, did not understand; he disobeyed, reversed the balance of his nature, and so brought himself and his posterity under the same law as that which rules the beasts that perish. That meant he could no longer develop as he ought; the landslide of his revolt and separation from the Source of life had carried away the straight though uphill road to his perfection, and there was no other. To take another figure, he was now a caterpillar that must turn chrysalis, but could not hatch.

Thus human death and all that goes with it was not so much a punishment for sin as its inevitable consequence. There was nothing vindictive in its imposition, for there can never be vindictiveness in Love. Rather, it was a remedial penalty, designed from the first to destroy at the last the very evil that had brought it into being. For there was no suspension of God's purpose, no going back on his creative word, 'Let us make Man in our own image.' When his work was broken, he stooped at once to build it up again. So, in the very context of the Fall, beside that first intolerable glimpse of human shame, we find the cryptic, embryonic promise that is called *Protevangelium*, the First Good News. The serpent shall bruise the heel of the seed of the woman whom he led astray; but the seed of the woman shall bruise the serpent's head. The word 'bruise' represents a Hebrew verb that might be rendered 'grind'; such injuries to head and heel respectively are far from fifty–fifty. A fight is on, we are assured, in which both parties will get hurt; but Man will be the outright winner in the end.

14

FROM ADAM TO THE FLOOD

IF you believe that Man's beginning took place in all essentials as Genesis asserts, then you will naturally want to know what happened between Adam and the earliest recorded history in which your own forebears played any part. The Jewish compilers of Genesis in about the fifth century BC felt just the same; and, being unembarrassed by our modern knowledge of Man's vast antiquity and undisturbed by slight discrepancies, they filled the gap with two ancient traditions of the descent of Noah, the forebear of their father Abraham, through only six or seven intermediate generations from one or other of the sons of Adam.[1] That retrospect is perfectly correct in that it shows mankind continuing from Adam to the writer's present day, but it is most enormously foreshortened. Let us try now to get some notion of the real time-gap.

Suppose you have a reel of paper, like a roll of tickets, but marked off in inches like a tennis marker. Suppose further that each inch stands for a thousand years—ten centuries and about forty generations—of the existence of the human race on earth. On this scale less than two inches of this strip will take you back to Christ, less than another two to Abraham; less than two more, and you have got to Noah, on the middle of the fourth millennium BC. The total thus far is not yet six inches. To reach the beginning of Neolithic times, the New Stone Age, however, it seems that you must add another eighteen inches straight away; and to get even to the end of the Palaeolithic—that is, to

the point in time when the European ice ages set in—you
have got to make your whole strip about six hundred
inches, which equals fifty feet or nearly seventeen yards.
Six hundred thousand years is over half a million; and
even then, although your strip of paper had now unrolled
itself out of your room and half way down the passage,
you have still not got to the beginning of the human race.
For even a whole million years ago, at the beginning of the
Pleistocene or period of most recent life, there were, apparently, at least four different types of Man, four separate
species of the genus *Homo*, already in existence. To trace
the river of humanity back to the common source whence
all the species sprang, we must look so much further back
that a strip of half a mile might still be short.

There is plenty of room in that uncharted past for the
world ages of world-wide tradition with their recurrent
rhythm, and plenty of evidence in the earth itself that they
did actually occur. And though the mind may reel before
the thought of such a vast pre-history, the believing heart
must marvel at four quite certain facts. Consider what
these are.

1. Each individual human pedigree goes back right
through those ages to the single source. At every moment
in them you and I had ancestors alive somewhere on earth.

2. Men died from the beginning, as well as multiplied,
and went on doing both. Within the first few generations
the number of human beings lodged *pro tempore* in death
must have exceeded that of those alive on earth. What the
proportion of that chrysalis part of Man is to the caterpillar
portion *now* one simply cannot think. But dead men are
still bits of Man, no less than you and I. God the Creator
speaks no idle word; those he has called to be still are, and
like ourselves await the consummation of his purpose for
the whole.

3. God's image was defaced in Man by Adam's fall, but

78

it was not destroyed, although men went on sinning; nor was all quite forgotten that had been learnt in Eden. Death was still dimly felt to be unnatural for Man, and not the end of him. There was always some belief, however crude, in powers or a Power greater and other than Man, yet all around him and determining his life. And God, who will not break the bruised reed nor quench the smoking flax, cherished those sparks in Man.

4. You will remember that, right up to the moment of Man's creation, what we may now call the *ekklēsia* principle was operating to bring him into being. There was the choice of Earth for the abode of life; then, from the varied forms of life, God set aside the primates, the direct succession that should lead to Man, and finally, if our conjecture on page 68 may be allowed, there was the calling out of the one sub-human individual, from whom by a direct creative act the Holy Spirit brought the Man who was the Church, God's chosen and his own. And now, in these dark ages of pre-history that followed on the Fall, we find God working on the same selective principle *within mankind itself*. For out of those four human species of which we spoke just now, one only has survived; all the existing races of mankind today, whether white, black, brown or yellow and from Congo pygmy to Ruwanda giant, are sub-species of the species *Homo sapiens*. Neandertal and Pekin and Rhodesian man seem to have disappeared from the face of the earth thousands of years before recorded history began. They were men too, though primitive, and as such are included surely in the many sons our Maker wills to bring to glory; but they were not his chosen instrument for bringing that general beatitude to pass. They were not the human primates, through whom the Second Adam was to trace his ancestry; and *Homo sapiens* was. Thus in the survival of the species to which we all belong we have the first indication in human history that

79

an *ekklēsia*, a people called and chosen from among all others, was to be God's agent for redeeming all.

The Biblical writers, however, knew nothing of any human species but their own. The first clear demonstration of the *ekklēsia* principle in Scripture is in the story of Noah and the Flood.[2]

We overleap long ages to arrive at Noah, for when he steps upon the scene the central point of human history, to which all has been leading since the Fall, is relatively near. What the Bible calls *The* Flood, using a special word, was a local Mesopotamian catastrophe in the fourth millennium BC. There are various theories about its cause. In Genesis it appears at first sight to be a river flood caused by excessive rain. But in 6.17 and 7.6 we should probably read, not 'Behold, I do bring the flood *of waters—hammabbûl mayim*—on the earth', but 'Behold, I do bring the flood *from the sea—ham-mabbûl miyām*—upon the earth.' 'The flood from the sea' would then be a tidal wave, originating in the seismic arc around the Andaman Islands, and diverted, probably by winds also of seismic origin, up the narrows of the Persian Gulf to overwhelm the Land of the Two Rivers, themselves in flood already from the heavy rains that often go with such disturbances. That seems the likeliest explanation, on the whole, of that unprecedented inundation. There is no doubt whatever that it did take place. Sir Leonard Woolley found the mud it left behind under three later occupation levels at ancient Ur, and dug down through eight solid feet of it to the drowned neolithic village underneath.

Disaster, then, about six thousand years ago, befell a portion of the human race, and wiped it out almost entirely. And once again, as in those dim traditions of the great catastrophe from which the earth we know was born, the enemy of Man, the hostile force, was water. Therein lies the primary significance of Noah. He and his family experienced and survived a cataclysm on the pattern of the Creation story of their ancestors. Through that local Flood, in circumstances that bit it deep into their minds, one family, called out by God, relearnt the ancient lesson in their own experience and relived the archetypal pattern of the saving Work of God.

And their experience had features which the earlier had lacked, exciting details that make one feel how things are speeding up at last—if one may reverently use the word— towards that crowning saving Act of God, that should at once fulfil and utterly surpass all types. Mountain tops had been the only hope for Noah's ancestors, and that is why you find God worshipped on high mountains and called in Ps. 18, verse 1 by that lovely string of refuge epithets, one of which comes from a root meaning 'to be inaccessibly high'—that is, out of reach of the destroying waters. But Noah and his family found refuge in the Ark, a house, a home, a ship, that floated safely on and amid the waters and eventually came unscathed to land. There is development, too, at the conclusion of the narrative, when the chosen family, the sole surviving remnant in the area, emerges from the Ark, together with their stock. Noah's first act then is to offer sacrifice to God, to whom they owe their preservation; and God accepts the sacrifice, and enters into covenant with Noah. So life in the Land between the Rivers, which for this family is all the earth they know, begins again, but with a difference. Together with a renewal of the primal blessing given to man and woman when they were first created, they now receive God's promise that this Flood, *the* Flood, shall be the last, and his 'bow in the cloud', that arches over all, becomes henceforth the token that this covenant in fact includes the earth in its entirety.

15

THE FIRST CHURCH

THE oldest living thing in the world today is the giant sequoia, known as 'General Sherman', in the Sequoia Park in California. A quite moderate estimate of its age puts it at about four thousand years. It must have been a sapling of a century or two when God called Abraham the Semite from his home and people, and 'Abraham went'.[1] So relatively recent is that far beginning of the first *ekklēsia* conscious of itself as such.

Self-conscious, conscious of direct divine vocation that must not be gainsaid, and with a forward look. Like his forefather Noah, Abraham received from God the primal blessing with a promise added; but whereas that to Noah had been negative, 'I will not destroy', the promise that God gave to Abraham was positive: 'I will bless you . . . and in you all the families of the earth shall be blessed.' Like the rainbow arching over all the earth, shedding its divers rays, seen and unseen alike, of the one perfect light upon the whole, this new Good News from God embraces all mankind. It tells us in plain words at last that his selective purpose has a collective, all-embracing end.

If you have a piece of rope, and someone ties a knot in it where no knot ought to be, the only way to get it out and straighten the rope is to pass the loops back in the reverse direction from that in which they went when it was tied.[2] The Fall of Man, as we have seen, consisted in two things—his failure to trust God and his resulting disobedience to God's known will. The chance that God gave

Abraham to reverse that sinful movement of Man's will was so momentous that the very heavens must have held their breath to see what he would do. By his obedience, when he could not know what hung upon his choice, Abraham became the physical ancestor of the Chosen People and so of the Incarnate Word, and the spiritual father of *all* them that believe. Italics mine; that 'all' is more inclusive than we incline to think, and no one can assess the debt we owe our father Abraham. So let us think a little about how he came to be the rock man that he was, the Peter of the First Ekklesia.

Consider first his background and environment. He appears in Genesis as a pastoral nomad with city connections; he probably acquired those through trade. The city whence he was first called was Ur, on the lower Euphrates; and Ur was a theocratic city-state—that is to say, a kingdom in which country, city and temple were a series of narrowing concentric circles centred on the God who, through the king and priesthood, determined all the state's activities. That Ur was already decadent in Abraham's time is immaterial; the important thing is that he knew its social pattern and formed a part of it. For the same pattern, reappearing after a thousand years in the Jerusalem of Abraham's seed, is taken thence in the New Testament to typify the heavenly consummation of our human destiny.

Men being what they are, we may well think that things in ancient Ur were less ideal than this God-centred polity of theirs suggests. Nevertheless, the worship at Ur, as also at Harran, whither Abraham migrated, was that of the Moon God, the loftiest form of faith that then obtained. The Moon God was regarded as the Father of his people, and one of his chief attributes was mercy. This belief seems to be enshrined—and O how fitly for the instrument of mercy that he was!—in Abraham's own name; for this in both its forms is probably a form of *Abi-ramu*, My-Father-is-merciful. And it appears that the moon who guides night-travelling nomads on their dangerous way was worshipped by the pastoral Semites too. Thus God, who like a wise and thrifty housewife always makes do and mends, in making Abraham just what he was by race and period gave him the best foundation of belief about himself that then existed, and gave it him in double strength. And just as Abraham's link with the Sumerian temple-states furnished the pattern for Man's final goal, so did his traditional nomadic life provide the figure for the earthly pilgrimage towards the heavenly goal.

That, then, was Abraham's background and the equipment with which he started out. Consider next the discipline God put him through, on the *Chi* principle. First he required him to have and to maintain complete faith in himself both in regard to the initial order to leave home and country, not knowing whither he went, and in regard to the promise of seed which, as the years went by, must have seemed more and more unlikely ever to be fulfilled. The incident of Hagar[3] shows how the Enemy's 'You will . . . not die!' (whispered to Sarah first, you notice, as formerly to Eve) had tortured him, and had even to some extent and for a time prevailed; but there was a severer test to come. A test, an ordeal both to prove and to increase his faith, and so to fit him for his place in God's economy, that is the meaning of the story in Gen. 22. Abraham must have been familiar with human sacrifice, for at Harran a white-faced man was offered to the Moon-God every year, the formula of oblation being 'We offer thee that which resembles thee.'[4] He would see it as the giving of the utmost best to God, at utmost cost; his best above all price was Isaac, that child of promise given at long last on whom alone, apparently, God's further promise of blessing through his seed for all mankind depended.

84

And Abraham believed *in* God, even for that; and Jewish tradition is emphatic that Isaac also was willing to be offered, for he too trusted God.

Our Lord said nineteen centuries later, 'Your father Abraham was overjoyed to see my day; he saw it, and was glad.'[5] Was it on Mount Moriah that he saw it, when his knife was stayed?

Consider next the strange theophany to Abraham's grandson Jacob at the ford of Jabbok.[6] When deadly peril threatened him, in consequence of his past sin against his brother, 'Jacob was left alone, and a man wrestled with him until the breaking of the day'—a Man who, because Jacob would not otherwise leave hold of him, both lamed and blessed him, changing his name to Israel, God-persists, because Jacob had striven and prevailed *with God*. There are great depths of mystery here, but one thing surely we may take as certain. A man prevails with God when he takes the discipline God lays on him, however much he suffers in the struggle. Jacob as well as Abraham was a key man for the work of salvation, one of the primates whence the Saviour was to spring. When he also responded, then indeed the day was breaking, and the climax of God's age-long persistence in his purpose was at hand.

In Part I we gave two chapters to the remaining history of this First Church, the children of the Israel who thus prevailed with God. Here, therefore, we need only to remind ourselves of three great crises in that history, which link up what has gone before in this inquiry with what is yet to come.

The first is the long complex of events, which began when Israel and his family went down to Egypt and ended with their return to Canaan, the home that none of the returned had ever seen before. That crisis centred on the Great Deliverance from Egypt, by sacrifice and Sea, that

85

culminated in the covenant at Sinai, by which the tribes of Israel were sealed and separated as God's peculiar People in whom he was pleased to dwell. The Chosen People themselves, when they looked back on that experience, saw in it a new saving Act of God, on the Creation pattern. And St Paul says that those things happened to them *typikos*, by way of types.[7] That is to say, they both happened on the pattern of a former saving Act of God, and themselves foreshadowed a greater yet to come.

The second crisis was the settlement in Canaan, which brought with it three changes in their way of life. They became settled farmers, and from association with other agricultural tribes acquired the idea of God as Husband of his People which, as I tried to show in Chapter 12, really results from Man's creation in his image. Further, this people whose constitution had hitherto been patriarchal, became a theocratic city-state in which God was represented both by the sacred person of the king and—in lieu of an image—by the Ark of the Covenant that had been brought from Sinai. And lastly, Israel's hope for the future, based on the promise to Abraham that he should be a blessing for all the families of earth, was by a special revelation to David, the founder of the royal house, focused on his line. From that time onwards Israel's hope of salvation to come centred on an individual anointed king of David's family.

The third and final crisis was the series of events that produced and followed the prophetic ministry of the Second Isaiah. From Babylon, whither the First Church had been exiled for her sins, he foresaw a return to Jerusalem, together with a more than restoration of all that had been lost; and he saw it as a greater Great Deliverance and new Creation, the supreme and final saving Act of God. The fact that the actual return to the earthly Jerusalem proved a disappointment, and that the rebuilt temple had neither Ark nor king to symbolise its indwelling Lord, showed that the real fulfilment both of those prophecies and of the previous types was still to come. And Second Isaiah prophesied of more even than that. His was the vision also of the Suffering Servant of the Lord. 'Servant of Yahweh' was a royal title; the Servant of that vision is king and priest and victim all in one, he wins his kingdom by the sacrificial death he suffers at his subjects' hands. Thus he not only embodies all that wrestling Jacob stood for in the way of man's acceptance of God's saving and life-giving discipline, and sublimates the whole idea of sacrifice; he also shadows forth the fact, for which God's earlier dealings also have prepared us, that God intends to use one man to save all Man.

So from that peak of prophecy we may now overleap the intervening centuries, and come to her whose Son the Saviour was.

16

THE SECOND MAN

'ALL things are double one against another, and He hath made nothing imperfect.'[1] In the perfect work of God in our creation and redemption this doubleness itself is double: there is the doubleness of paradox, the two sides of the truth that contradict and yet complete each other; and there is also what may be termed inclusively the doubleness of correspondence. I say inclusively, because this doubleness itself is of three kinds. There is first the doubleness of symbol or analogy, as when the Kingdom of Heaven is likened unto this or that familiar earthly thing with which it corresponds. Then there is the doubleness of type and the event or person typified, as with the whole complex of Israel's Exodus from Pharaoh's and the devil's tyranny. And lastly, there is the doubleness of actual persons of corresponding function in God's plan, namely, the First and Second Adam and the First and Second Eve.

The Second Eve presents us with another doubleness. The salient facts about the Eve of Genesis were these: first, she was taken out of Adam and was posterior to him in time; second, she met temptation first and afterwards by him became the mother of all living. In the corresponding series this order is reversed, for the Second Adam is himself the seed of the woman. So Eve has two fulfilments. The first in time was Mary of Nazareth, who gave him birth; the second was the Second Church, his Bride, the help-meet for him, born from his pierced side.

Consider Mary as the Second Eve. In Gabriel's message

88

she encountered a challenge to her faith greater than that at which her prototype had failed, harder and even more momentous than the one her father Abraham had taken up. It is striking that in her acceptance of it she calls herself 'the servant of the Lord', the title of the Second Isaiah's Servant with the gender changed.[2] With her, the words were simply the expression of absolute surrender to God's will; nevertheless Mary *was* royal, both as David's daughter and as the chosen mother of Messiah; and her vocation from the first involved the greatest suffering on her Son's account. Never has he rebuked and chastened any whom he loves as he rebuked and chastened his own blessed mother; nowhere is the *Chi* principle more clearly seen than in her case.

Mary is thus the Second Eve, in that she met the crucial testing before the Second Adam; she is the Second Eve also, in that as his mother she is the mother also of all who live by him. Leaving the other Second Eve to be considered later, let us now think about our Lord as Second Adam.

He is actually called the Second Adam only by St Paul in 1 Corinthians; but the apostle is not innovating in so calling him, for all the Gospels time and again present him as the Second Man implicitly. It will be worth our while to think this out a little, taking the Gospel story under five main heads.

First, as to our Lord's conception, birth and infancy. St Luke, in narrating his birth of a woman and tracing his ancestry through Abraham to Adam, shows him to be that promised seed of the woman, who should grind the serpent's head. In recording that his mother conceived him, while she was yet a virgin, by the power of the Holy Spirit, he shows him as unique, sole of his kind *as Man*, even apart from his unique divinity. The angel's words to Mary at the Annunciation are most striking; he tells her that 'the holy *Thing* that is being begotten shall be called son of God'.[3] St Luke calls Adam also 'son of God'. What God himself assumed of the Virgin Mary was not just one man's body, but humanity; manhood was then recreated by a new Act of God.

The emphasis in St Luke, as also in St Matthew as far as he goes, is thus on the fact that Jesus is true Man and new Man. In the Fourth Gospel his Godhead is stressed: it is the Word, by whom all things were made, who thus takes flesh. But that very fact sets the Incarnation against the background of Creation; this Gospel begins as Genesis begins, 'In the beginning . . .'; the Word himself is the link between that creation and the present, for he was in the beginning and now he is made flesh, his incarnation corresponding to the uplifting of the Earthborn, Adam, into a living soul.

Nor is that all. 'He came unto his own, and his own received him not.' Even before he left his mother's womb, the serpent was bruising the heel of the seed of the woman. There was no room in the inn for his birth at Bethlehem, and his very life was threatened before he was two years old. And then the Second Man was exiled from his rightful home, as was the First.

Consider next his Baptism and Temptation. He was baptised *into* Jordan.[4] 'Into' implies immersion; he let the waters meet over his head. In bowing thus beneath the hostile waters, the Second Adam showed that he was undertaking the ordeal by battle proper to the First. But water also cleanses, and indeed is a necessity for life,[5] and symbolises it; and the Baptism of John was a baptism of repentance, a symbolic cleansing of the penitent. So our Lord's acceptance of it showed that he was shouldering the guilt of the First Adam too. And further, as the Fathers loved to teach, he cleansed the waters by thus entering them; so that, as we shall see in the next chapter, they might become the sacramental channel of the forgiveness and new life that the new Man was setting out to make available for all the members of the old.

On his emergence from the water he received the anointing of the Holy Spirit, who appeared in the form of a dove. There are two contacts there with Genesis: the Spirit brooded, bird-like,[6] over the primaeval chaos; a dove was the evangelist to Noah in his re-experience of the Creation pattern. With the outpouring of the Spirit came the Father's voice, authenticating Jesus as his Son, both human and divine, and as his Servant, who should redeem Man by his death.[7]

The conflict symbolised by the immersion in Jordan was actualised forthwith in the Temptation. The First Man was tempted in a garden, the Second in a wilderness—an apt exchange, considering what the First has made of God's good earth. The First was tempted through the serpent; but disguises are off when 'He is among the wrestlers who as God awards the prizes'; it is the devil, the author of evil, in his own person who assaults the Second Man.[8] St Mark states the fact only of the Temptation, with the one significant detail that in the wilderness the Lord 'was with the wild beasts'—the beasts that surely were not wild with him and never would have been so at all, had the First Man fulfilled his stewardship in their regard. St Matthew and St Luke describe a threefold temptation, which in St Luke's order corresponds with the threefold temptation of Eve to 'the lust of the flesh, the lust of the eyes, and the pride of life'. And the forty days of his fast further recalls the period of the Flood.

Thirdly, there is the Ministry. As we noted in Part I, p. 18, the immediate background against which our Lord appears in the Synoptic Gospels is the Second Isaiah's prophecies of the Return of God's exiled People to Jerusalem; thus John the Baptist is the voice that cries for the homeward road to be prepared, and Jesus is by implication the Bringer of Good News to Sion, the first of the returning people to come home. But this new Great Deliverance of the prophet's vision is itself (as also we noted) on the pattern of the initial saving Act of God in the creation of the world from chaos. Further, the state of exile that required such an act was an element in the situation that went back directly, behind the intervening exile of Israel in Egypt, to Man's exile from Eden; for the exile in Babylon was, like that from Eden, a punishment for sin, which the Egyptian one was not. So once again we find ourselves led back to Genesis and the First Man for the conceptions in the light of which we must interpret Jesus.

And even if we overlooked all that, our Lord's own title for himself would tell us who he is. He called himself *the Son of Man*, taking the Aramaic term from Dan. 7, where one like to a Son of Man comes and is brought to the Ancient of Days in heaven. The term means *The* Man, the real Man,[9] and in Daniel's vision this real Man appears as such in contrast to the beasts. The parallel with the First Man could not be clearer; here is the Second Man, the genuine, the only rational.

'As it is written that the First Man Adam was made a living soul, so was the Last Adam made a life-giving spirit.' That essential contrast which St Paul makes between the two is embodied in all our Lord's manward activities, and is what we called in Chapter 12 the ultimate reality of gender. Jesus is Masculinity incarnate; he gives. The members of the First Man, with whom he deals, receive. He gives health to the sick, sight to the blind, hearing to the deaf, speech to the dumb, power to the paralysed, freedom to be themselves to the possessed, and life to the dead. He speaks with absolute authority. And it is not only men who thus receive from him. The wind takes orders from him, the sea supports his feet, water becomes wine, and food is multiplied.

Now, fourthly, for the peak point of his life, his Transfiguration.[10] It is difficult to emphasise sufficiently the centrality of this event. We learnt from Genesis that human death resulted from Man's sin; if he had not sinned, he would not have died. That much was clear; but nothing positive was told us as to the way in which he would have developed if he had not sinned. Now in the Second, the Last Adam on the mount we see what would have happened, we see the ultimate perfection that God intends for Man. No physical deterioration, no rending of the earthly body from the soul, but metamorphosis,[11] as smooth as sunrise, into the full-grown Man. That was what Adam's uphill journey would have led him to, if he had stood the rigours of the way. Thither the Second Adam's uphill journey actually did lead him; and perfected Man stood on an earthly mountain-top, and was seen by the mortal eyes of Peter, James and John.

He took the human glory that was natural to him as Man not only negatively sinless, but positively wholly given to God in creaturely dependence. He laid that glory down again of his own will, reverting to his larval state, that in a larval, mortal body he might suffer the death that sin had brought on the entire First Man, and turn it from a *cul de sac* into the way to life.

This brings us to the Passion of the Second Man, and its triumphant issue in the Resurrection. In that complex event everything that the Baptism of Jesus had foreshadowed was finally fulfilled. It was the last round of the battle between the Strong and the Stronger than he;[12] and I would like to remark in passing that, though that parable recalls the story of David and Goliath, which did indeed typify our Lord's victory over Satan,[13] the *first* time in human history that that act was staged, the first occasion

93

when the Enemy was given a man, that they might fight together, was in the Garden of Eden; but then the duel went the other way. And that is why there came a Second Adam to the fight. That fight was centred in the hours on the Cross, which by its very shape and name recalls the principle of testing that obtains in all creation, and by its substance links us with that other tree, that was the occasion of the First Man's sin. And the centre of the hours on the Cross, the crisis of the God-Man's wrestling with God for Man's salvation, is the dereliction; and we know of that unfathomable mystery because, when it was over, he himself spoke of it in the words of the twenty-second Psalm:

My God, my God, why didst thou forsake me?[14]

We should consider this first half-verse in connection with the rest of the Psalm, and most particularly with certain phrases in the last three verses:

The kingdom is the Lord's.
. . . . .
All they that go down to the dust shall kneel before
  him:
  even he whose soul is not alive.
They shall come, and shall declare his righteousness
  unto a People that shall be born,
  that he has acted.

The first clause states a present fact, the issue of the Second Adam's victory. Those that follow are prospective, and they contain three reminiscences of Gen. 2.7.

(i) 'All they that go down to the dust', all those who, because of sin, must return to the dust whence they were formed at the first, all the men who make up the First Man.

(ii) The next clause is literally, 'Even he whose *nephesh* is not *ḥayyah*'—i.e. whose soul is no longer living as it was

94

when Man was made, for it has come under the law of death.

(iii) The verb in the last clause is absolute, without an object. It means 'to make', as well as 'to act' or 'to do', and it is the same verb as that translated 'formed'—'the Lord God formed the Man'—in the aforesaid verse of Genesis. 'That he has acted' implies therefore that he has done a new creative act.

We said at the beginning of this chapter that the Eve of Genesis had two fulfilments, and that the first was Mary, the Second Adam's mother. The other Second Eve, the Second and Last Church that is potentially renewed humanity, was the new creation made on Calvary. Our Lord had said that he had come to earth to perfect his Father's work, and in the Sixth Word from the Cross he said of that same Work, 'It has been perfected.' Because he died that she might live, we can truly say that God took this new Eve from the new Adam's side as he slept the sleep of death, and know her therefore as truly bone of his bones and flesh of his flesh, created from him, posterior to him, to be his Bride, an answering help for him. And paradoxically she was at the moment of her creation both the Church without spot or wrinkle, ready for union with himself, and the People that should be born, the People that should begin its active and empowered life only at Pentecost and that today still waits her perfecting.

We shall revert to this subject of the Second Church in the next chapter. One thing only remains to mention in this present one, with reference to our Lord as Second Adam; and that is at once the most important and the most impossible to talk about—namely, the Resurrection.

We mostly think of the Resurrection as the Father's vindication of the Son, the manifestation of the triumph and glory that were hidden on the Cross. It was all that; and it was also the re-assumption by the sinless Second

Man of that ultimate perfection proper to human nature, which he had first assumed in the Transfiguration. When he thus reassumed it finally, he was not only seen by Peter, James and John, but seen and heard and touched and handled in that perfect state by several hundred people.[15] For six weeks of spring-time nearly nineteen centuries ago perfected Man was seen and loved on this same earth that the unfallen Adam, the germinal Man, had walked millions of years before, and that we live on now. At will he showed himself, at will he was unseen. He consorted with his friends, and went for walks, and shared a supper, and picnicked by the lake. Nothing could have been homelier, nothing more natural. For it *was* natural; that is the point. And his sole Resurrection from the unnumbered myriads of the dead is the pledge and proof that the road to Man's natural perfection once more lies open to all the sons of men.

Christ the Firstfruits; and afterwards they that are Christ's, at his Coming.[16]

THE SECOND CHURCH

THE work of the First Man's redemption and remaking
was by the Second Adam's death on Calvary in one sense
perfected and in another sense begun. There is a hint of
the same paradox in the Eve of Genesis. She was created
bone of Adam's bones and flesh of his flesh, and derived
her being from him; but the very purpose of her creation
was that she might *become* his wife, and enter into a further
oneness of flesh and more than flesh with him in the union,
not of unconscious origin but of conscious, willing love.
The Church that was born of the Second Adam on the
Cross has also to become what she already is; that becom-
ing is the business of these Last Days, until he comes to
claim her. But before we consider the means by which this
process is effected, we must think a little about the scope
of the redemption and recreation of which she is the agent
for mankind.

Our Lord wrestled and prevailed on Calvary as and for
Man, *all* Man. What he did there had reference not only
to the small portion of mankind then living on the earth,
nor even only to the living and the generations yet unborn,
among whom we then were. It looked back too, covering
the whole race from its source. And after death he went,
himself discarnate, to tell the Good News to all the spirits
in prison,[1] all those unthinkable millions of the First
Adam, who also had laid off their mortal bodies.

And the redeeming work of Jesus went beyond even the
utmost confines of humanity. Already in his mother's

womb he had recapitulated the whole evolutionary process from the single cell to Man, thus touching life at every level.[2] Crowned in his Passion with a crown of thorns, the symbol of the curse in which the earth was implicated by the First Man's fall,[3] he had removed the curse. And even with the earth we have not reached the limit. As we observed in Chapter 12, you cannot say where Man's connections with creation stop; he is a cosmic creature and our Lord, in taking manhood, took the universe. St Paul expresses this in Romans 8 by saying, 'For the creation waits with eager longing for the revealing of the sons of God.'[4] Venantius Fortunatus voices the same thought in the *Lustra sex*:

> From that holy Body broken
> Blood and water forth proceed;
> Earth and stars and sky and ocean
> By that flood from stain are freed.

We have some sort of an illustration of this quite literally universal scope of the redemption in the rainbow, that token of God's covenant with Noah which to all time remains the symbol of his faithfulness. Made by the sunlight that has come through heaven to earth, it arches over earth as its immediate sphere; but, like all light that earth or any heavenly body either receives or gives, this light also streams outward into space. Further, in passing through earth's watery atmosphere—and mark the element—the single perfect light is broken up into its several parts. Of these the human eye sees seven colours only; but the unseen ultra-violet and infra-red light-rays act secretly and ceaselessly upon all life. So, since the Sun of Righteousness arose with healing in his wings, his varied light has been at work upon his whole creation. And even in its operation on mankind on earth there is always immeasurably more to it than we can ever see.

It is against that cosmic background, which people usually ignore, that we must try to see the Second Church.

The Second Church was the continuation of the First, as well as a new creation; for the first Christians were all Jews, reborn as members of the New Man Christ. We commonly call Pentecost the birthday of the Christian Church, because the Holy Spirit then came upon the hundred and twenty. But babes are not born talking, and the Church of Pentecost was nothing if not vocal. Her Bethlehem was surely Calvary, where (as we said) she issued from her Adam's side; and Pentecost, the promised baptism with fire and the Holy Spirit, answers in her experience to his divine anointing and authentication at the baptism of John. And she was given and still has that unction of the Spirit to the same end as he. From Jordan he was driven by the Spirit into the wilderness to meet the Enemy; thence to the ardours of the ministry; thence to his death, and by death to the ultimate perfection for which Man was made. We in the Church on earth receive the Holy Spirit, that we in Christ may travel by Christ's road to the same goal.

In the great passage of which we quoted part at the beginning of this Part, St Paul sums up the matter thus:

'There is one Body and one Spirit, just as you were called to the one hope that belongs to your call, one Lord, one faith, one baptism, one God and Father of us all who is above all, and through all, and in all. But grace was given to each of us according to the measure of Christ's gift. Therefore it is said:

' "When he ascended on high he led a host of captives, and he gave gifts to men . . ."

'And his gifts were that some should be apostles, some prophets, some evangelists, some pastors and teachers, for the equipment of the saints, for the work

99

of ministry, for building up the Body of Christ, until we all attain to the unity of faith and of the knowledge of the Son of God, to mature manhood, to the measure of the stature of the fulness of Christ.'[5]

From this superbly comprehensive statement three things emerge of special relevance here.

First, there is the fact we have already mentioned that the Church, the New Humanity, is not yet full-grown. This is so enormously important and so largely overlooked at the present day that we must be forgiven if we rub it in. We, living on this earth, are larval creatures; those who have died, no matter how long ago, are larval still, in the pre-final stage of metamorphosis. *The First Man as a whole* is only adolescent. The only full-grown Man, to date, is Jesus Christ. But his full-grownness is the pledge of that of all mankind. When he blotted out the writ of our condemnation, nailing it to his cross, he made it possible for the First Adam also to grow up. The same adulthood that men would have reached if they had never sinned is possible again for them, and even certain; but because of sin they have to reach it by a different road. *Resurrection IS Transfiguration, reached through death.*

With the apostles, who had met the full-grown Man, his resurrection was the heart and centre of the Gospel; indeed a main requirement for apostleship was to have seen him risen. For without the individual resurrection of the Second Adam there is no resurrection for the First; the Fall has not been reversed, death is frustration, and God's original purpose for mankind can never be fulfilled. But glory be to God, Christ *has* been raised, and by that fact the ultimate resurrection of all the dead is guaranteed. And when the dead have risen, they will be full-grown. Those, therefore, who say that the resurrection of the body is a crude, material belief untenable by spiritual and enlightened persons are talking the most insensate nonsense that ever issued from the mouth of man.

We have left Ephesians and gone to 1 Corinthians, to clinch this argument; and it has taken us beyond the past and present to the end of time. We had to do this, because the general resurrection of mankind is the next-to-the-coping-stone of revelation. I say 'next to', because the resurrection is not itself the consummation of all things, but only the essential prelude to it. In the Apocalypse the Church, mankind renewed in Christ, appears as the Bride made ready for her Bridegroom. She is called his wife in the same breath,[6] because in that last vision the marriage of the Lamb has actually come, and the union of Man with God, the ultimate reality of gender, is on the point of being realised. The resurrection precedes this consummation, because the Bride-Church is not nubile until she is full-grown, the Second Eve is not an helpmeet for the Second Adam till she is perfected, even as he.

Now we return to the Ephesians passage to think about two other of its implications that bear upon our theme.

The first—the second of the three—is this. The Church, the New Humanity, appears in it as made in the image of God even as Adam was, but on a higher plane. That is to say, she is at once individual and social, one Body made up of many members each with its own function; and she is also creative, in that by spiritual procreation she has to increase her membership till she is co-extensive with the former Man. It is thus of her essence that she should propagate her kind; and elsewhere St Paul speaks of himself as travailing in birth with souls.

This brings us to our final point, namely the Church's ministry and sacraments as God's appointed means by which she may become what she already is—that is to say, may come to full-grown Man. The ministry and sacraments are both expressions of the sacramental principle on which Man himself is made. Man is by constitution an embodied spirit; in him a body, formed from dust and destined to return to it since sin upset the balance, is linked with and expresses an immortal unseen soul. In the ministry spiritual treasures are given us through human channels; in the sacraments the unseen inward graces of the Spirit are mediated by analogous outward and visible signs.

The function of ministering life to others in one way or another belongs to the Church as a whole, as indeed on a lower plane it belongs to Man as a whole; no man lives or dies unto himself in either Christ or Adam. That interdependence is involved in our God-likeness, as we have already tried to show; and we shall revert to it in our concluding chapter. In the official ministry, however, the apostles and prophets and the rest whom St Paul here enumerates, and their successors in the later threefold ministry, the function of propagating and developing the life of the New Man in the sons of the old is exercised supremely; and in most cases the administration of the sacraments is reserved to them. Of these, only Baptism is actually mentioned in the passage under our consideration; but the other great sacrament of the Gospel, the Holy Eucharist, of which the function is to develop the life thus given in germ, is implicit in the emphasis on growth. Let us consider the relation of the elements in these two sacraments to the foregoing and forthcoming history of Man.

The element in Baptism is water—water in both its values. It is the hostile element; and that is properly denoted by the immersion of the catechumen in it. But it is also the cleansing and life-giving element; and, because Christ has conquered the Enemy once and for all, and has turned against him those weapons of suffering and death wherein he trusted,[7] the water of Baptism becomes, through the creative word that goes with it, the vehicle of cleansing and regeneration. Together with Confirmation, which is properly part of it, it is the individual's Pentecost.

In the Eucharist the elements are bread and wine, the all-sufficient basic elements of food and drink. These take us back to Eden. Man was not meant to be a carnivore; he was put to rule the animals, not to shed their blood. It was the vegetable creation that God appointed for his food, and, in accordance with the *Chi* principle that all growth comes through effort, he put him in a garden to grow it for himself. And bread and wine are doubly the fruit of man's labour with the God-given fruits of the earth; for they are the man-made products of cultivated plants.

Of course, it is not only the elements in the Eucharist that take us back to Eden. The institution of that Sacrament is the mid-point between the Creation and the Consummation. In a true sense it was for this that rationality was given, that human hands might bless and break the bread and bless and give the cup, that human lips, voicing a human will, might transmute even death by giving thanks for it. And equally, of course, there is much more that is significant about the Eucharistic elements than their connection with Eden; indeed, the whole Bible is implicit in them and in the Baptismal element of water. For instance, bread is made from wheat, that must fall to the ground and die in order to live, and is so unimaginably other in its full-grown form than in the dry, bare seed.[8] And wine is made by crushing grapes in the press; therefore it is a symbol of shed blood, of life out-poured, and links with all the history of bloody sacrifice, that never would have been, had the First Man not sinned, and culminates in the atoning death on Calvary. So bread and wine, by the Word's own creative word, are in this sacrament his body and his blood, first separate as in death and then united in the chalice, as in his resurrection; and they are given to the baptised for food, to make them grow, in body as in soul, into the perfect Man. *In body as in soul*. We Anglicans are happy to have that affirmed for us in the words of administration in the Book of Common Prayer. This earthly life is sometimes called a vale of soul-making, and such indeed it is; but for that very reason it is a vale of body-making too. Our resurrection bodies are being built up *now*. The sacraments are interim means of grace, ordained to suit our present undeveloped state; but the grace itself is given precisely to enable us to reach our full-grown state.

We must stress this stone, this next-to-the-coping-stone, of Christian faith yet once again. Man will continue both individual and social to all eternity. The births and deaths of individual men are scattered over time; but all their resurrections will occur together. *Man* will rise, not only certain men. But the individual risen bodies will not be mass-produced. The body of each one will be his own, unique, and it will show the person as he really is. It may well be that we are not wholly disembodied when we die; that the departing soul takes with it to the waiting state some of the substance of the mortal body to clothe it, be it never so tenuously, until the final change. If that is so, the resurrection body will issue from the interim form. In any case it will be the result, the ultimate inalterable consequence of its possessor's previous life. It is very striking that in the Parable of the Sheep and the Goats, which tells us what will happen at the Judgement, our Lord says nothing about evidence being given or witnesses called.[9] Surely the reason is that men's final bodies will be themselves both evidence and witnesses.

And after the Second Coming, the Resurrection and the

Judgement follows the Life Everlasting. *Life*. That is to be the *opus*; what comes before is only overture. And revelation does not go beyond the overture. The Apocalypse closes not with the actual marriage of the Lamb, but on the brink of it; when at long last the Bridegroom comes and takes his Bride to the wedding, the door is shut and we can see no farther. But even in the overture there are scraps of melody that hint at what will be developed in the work itself.

Man as created was the link between God and creation. When he sinned, he fell from his link-place, fell out of his right relationship with the animals and the earth and the heavens, as well as out of right relationship with God and into discord in himself; and so the universe was dislocated. It follows that the lower creatures have been arrested in their development and side-tracked from their goal, as well as Man himself; God may have meant him to lead them on through love to rationality. When the link is replaced at the final consummation what will ensue for them and for the rest of creation? It is very striking that in the Apocalypse the final scene is earth; the Bride comes down to earth from heaven for her wedding.[10] It seems that if the Church, as *kyriakon*, the Lord's Own, is then co-extensive with Man, and Man is once more one again with all creation, then all creation will in some sense be included in the Church;[11] and she, the feminine to God's eternal Masculine, will then be Catholic not only in the sense of man-wide, but literally universal, as co-extensive with the universe.

18

ON BEING HUMAN

EVERYTHING that we said in the closing chapter of Part I about the Practice of Expectation, of looking for the Consummation, applies here equally. But the theme of this book, together with the largely dehumanised state of our present civilisation, calls for a few reflections on being really human.

The word is commonly misused. A modern naturalist[1] has pointed out that much that we call human in the behaviour of the higher animals is really animal behaviour in ourselves. Further, you hear sin excused as 'only human' and 'quite natural'. But sin is really neither natural nor human; the whole point of the doctrine of Original Sin is that it was not original in the absolute sense; the stream was polluted after it gushed from the rock, and not before. So when Origen and St Bernard said that a man's first duty was to know himself, they meant (as we have said) that first and foremost he should recognise his own immeasurable dignity and worth, as a creature made in the image of God and loved by God. So we have first of all to be truly human in the way we regard ourselves; we have to love ourselves because God loves us and for the same reason. And we have to study to be truly human also in our relations with God, with our fellow men, and with the lower creation.

When you look at God's work in creation and redemption as a whole, as we have tried to do in this book, and see yourself as part of it, you cannot but be humbled to the dust by his humility and the immeasurable patience of his love. You are so loved, so rich; but you have nothing that he has not given you. That recognition of utter dependence and indebtedness, that reaction of entire faith and love and thankfulness to the Love that God is, is the only truly human attitude to God. And two things follow from it. First, you will know that you exist to serve God's purpose and to do his will, not *vice versa*; and second, you will take the discipline God lays on you. For it behoves a man, as man, to accept all forms of suffering and limitation, and supremely death, as penance for his own sins and the corporate sin of his race, in union with the Second Man's atoning death and with his glad and glorious thankfulness. Thus jibbing and self-pity are sub-human, and the most stunting sins; the truly human person, the consistent Christian, says 'Glory be to God for *all* things', as did St Chrysostom.

This cannot be emphasised too strongly. The whole principle of Redemption is that evil is to be made the instrument of its own overthrow. The business of life, the way to life, consists in getting over fences, not in lying down and moaning on the hither side.

As human beings, we are meant to be mirrors of God. That means that his humility and love and patience should be reflected in our relations with our fellow-men. A truly human life is an embodiment of the New Commandment, it reproduces the pen-portrait of the Second Man in 1 Cor. 13. But when our approach to others is *de haut en bas*, when we start from the assumption, conscious or otherwise, that we, or our Church, or our country are the Haves and everyone else the Have-nots in respect of faith or culture or what-not, we are being not human but devilish, for we are reflecting Satan's pride, not God's humility. Neither do we reflect God when we are stand-offish and keep ourselves to ourselves. The world is over-populated; but crowds are not communities, and, because so few of us are really human, loneliness is desperately common, and that not least sometimes in Christian households, for none can be so selfish as the pious. Here let us notice also that it is a great responsibility to have a face. You do not see your own face, but other people do; and your face is really made by the way you think. We have all met faces that did us good, and faces that did not; and in either case they might belong to strangers, who did not even know that we were looking at them.

Real humanness comes out also in the authentic quality of sympathy. The devil, who makes a speciality of counterfeits, encourages—and that not least among religious people—a pseudo-sympathy, an enervating kindness, the effect of which is to breed self-pity in the person on whom it is bestowed, and so to rob their suffering of its fruit. Parents and priests carry a tremendous responsibility here. It is so easy to mistake the false for the true when one's heart is wrung for a suffering child or soul. Again, no form of influence or authority is exercised humanly that is at all tinctured with totalitarianism; for such possessiveness violates both God's rights and the individual's. And—last but by no means least—the consistently human person will stand without any reservation for the sanctity of human marriage.

Thus far we have spoken only of our relations with other living members of our race; and their importance is indeed impossible to overestimate, for the individual exists to serve the body, and it is on 'You did it' or 'You did it not' in these relationships that we shall all be judged. But the really human person will remember that he is a member of Man, and that the vastly larger number of his brethren are waiting on the other side of death. We are so narrow in our thought of the departed. Even on All Souls' Day people think almost exclusively of those whom they have known in their own family or parish; and the prayer for the souls of the faithful departed is commonly restricted to departed Christians. The fulness of faith is indeed the unique possession of the Church, and one that none of us can ever fully realise; and much will be required from those to whom so very much is given. But it may well be questioned whether any men, even professed atheists, really believe in absolutely nothing; and there are elements so lofty in even the lowest forms of paganism that the resultant cultural and social patterns sometimes put our own to shame. And as far back as we have any knowledge of human faith at all, there is evidence at least of the belief that death for man was not the end. Some prehistoric peoples buried their dead in the foetal position, ready for new birth.[2] Even Neanderthal man interred his dead with care, putting red ochre on their bones, because blood is red and 'the life of the flesh is in the blood'.[3] Those were truly human actions. All men will stand together at the Judgement; all men should be included in our Christian prayers.

Thirdly, how will a truly human person regard the earth and all sub-human life? God has subjected it all to Man, for Man's good and its own; and Man has terribly betrayed and still betrays the trust. But God has not removed him from his stewardship; we are still as priests to the lower creation. The truly human person will be aware of this as part of his religion, and will want to make up both to God and to the earth and the creatures for the wrong his race has done and goes on doing. Even if he is not by temperament a lover of animals or plants, he can never be indifferent to them or to the earth on which they live. He will be sensitive to nature's metamorphoses and death and resurrection rhythms, and will regard all life with reverence, because God made it and it lives by him. But he will not spoil the animals he has to do with, for that is an abuse of stewardship only less great than being cruel to them. In the same way he will respect the earth and not exploit it. He will love it, and his reverent love for it and for the animals will be returned a thousandfold into his bosom; for God will give himself to him through them. The Lord God knew what he was about when he put the Man in a garden, to dress it and to till it; neither is it fortuitous that those who lead the contemplative life seek to support their prayer by working with their hands and on the land. We have got away from this in our urbanised modern life, and we have largely got away from God in consequence. We need to get back to it, and to its theological foundation. Our eternal future is bound up with that of all creation, and the *Chi* principle, that is the principle of Love, operates through all; not the Church, the full-grown Man, alone, but the whole universe will say at the Consummation, 'It is good for me that I have been in trouble.' We are all in it together, as the saying is.

Obviously none of us will get full marks in this examination in humanity, but it may perhaps have helped to show us where we stand. For our encouragement, let us conclude with two thoughts out of other people's books that help the writer of this one and may be helpful to its readers too.

The first is C. C. Torrey's explanation of the 'temptation' clause in the Lord's Prayer. He says[4] there is a verb in Aramaic (as there is in Hebrew) that means 'to enter' or 'go in', and also 'to succumb' or 'fail'. Whoever first translated the Lord's Prayer into Greek knew only the first meaning; and so, the verb here being causative in form, he rendered that petition, 'Lead us not—that is, suffer us not to enter—into temptation.' But what our Lord said was 'Let us not *fail* in temptation.' In the same way in Gethsemane he said to the three apostles, 'Awake and pray *that you may not fail in* temptation.' We have got to enter into testing and temptation, for there is no other

way of coming to the full-grown Man. But, thanks be to
the Second Adam, we have *not* got to fail!

The second thought comes from the same two fathers
whose teaching on self-knowledge we have already quoted,
and derives from their joint interpretation of these words
from the Song of Songs:

> Behold, there he stands
>> behind our wall,
>> gazing in at the windows
>> looking through the lattice.

For St Bernard, the wall is the flesh that hides our Lord
from us, yet is 'our' wall because God shares it with us; and
the apertures are the human senses through which he
gained experience of our needs and learned obedience by
the things he suffered. There is a lot to think about there,
but Origen has more. Where St Bernard's Latin version gave him 'lattices or windows', Origen, who used
the Greek, read 'nets'. And he equates these nets with the
psalmist's 'snares of the fowler', the temptations that the
devil lays across our paths to trip us up. But through these
same temptations our dear Lord himself looks out at us
and, finding him in them, we advance beyond them by
their means.

So, 'as in Adam all die, even so in Christ shall all be
made alive'. For that *Chi* principle is Love's one law for
bringing all things to perfection.

NOTES

PART I

INTRODUCTION

1. Dan. 7.

2. Dix, *The Shape of the Liturgy*, p. 262. See the whole section, pp. 256–67.

3. Rev. 22.13; cf. 1.8 and 21.6.

4. St Athanasius, *On the Incarnation of the Word of God*, section 7 (p. 33 in CSMV translation).

CHAPTER 1. HEAVEN

1. St Bernard, *On the Song of Songs*, Sermon XXIV.6.

2. St Athanasius, *op. cit.*, section 12.

3. Compare this passage from William of St Thierry, *Meditation VI*: 'For Thou, O Maker of all times and places, art neither moved by time nor limited by place; Thou art not held up in a material heaven lest Thou shouldest fall, nor dost Thou dwell therein in such a manner as not Thyself to fill both heaven and earth. For Thou art present everywhere, if one may use the word at all of Thee, Who art above all place; and everywhere Thou art in Thine entirety, if one may predicate entirety in or concerning Thee, Who knowest no division into parts. Yet Thou Thyself hast taught us to say, "Our Father, which art in heaven"; and this belief that God inhabits heaven is so general that all men hold it, even Jews and heathen.'

CHAPTER 2. THE COMING TYPIFIED

1. Both nouns have the article in the original Greek.

2. Luke 3.23–end.

3. Gen. 12.1–4 and 15.1–6.

4. See chiefly Exod. 1–20, 24, 31.18–34 end; Num. 10.29–14 end; Deut. 31–34; Josh. 1–4.

5. See e.g. Exod. 25.8, 29.45; Num. 5.3.

6. *Tehôm = Tiam*, *-at* being the feminine suffix.

CHAPTER 3. THE COMING PROPHESIED

1. The whole of Isa. 40–55 should be read, and also 35.

2. The suggestion is Dr Lowther Clarke's, in *Divine Humanity*, p. 91.

3. The noun has the definite article in Hebrew, which suggests that Ahaz would know to whom Isaiah was referring.

4. The Servant Songs are Isa. 42.1–4 or 9, 49.1–6, 50.1–9 or 11, 52.13–53.12.

5. Isa. 45.8.

CHAPTER 4. ON INSPIRATION AND BELIEVING IN THE HOLY SPIRIT

1. See Hoskyns and Davey, *The Riddle of the New Testament*, pp. 115ff. (This reference is to the first edition.)

2. Isa. 40.3; Mal. 3.1.

3. Luke 3.1–6.

4. John 1.1–18.

5. See Hoskyns and Davey, *op. cit.*, pp. 35–43.

6. See C. C. Torrey, *Our Translated Gospels*, pp. 2 and 87.

CHAPTER 5. FROM HEAVEN: INTO HEAVEN

1. Matt. 1 and 2; Luke 1 and 2.

2. John 1.11. The first 'His own' is neuter plural, the second masculine plural. He came to his own belongings, his own creation, and his own people received him not.

3. See Luke 11.14–22.

4. 1 Sam. 17.

5. Hos. 1–3; Jer. 3.14; Isa. 54.5; cf. also Isa. 62.5.

6. Mark 2.19; Matt. 9.15; Luke 5.34; Matt. 22.1–14, 25.1–13.

7. For example, St Augustine, *On St John cxx.2* (pp. 517f. in vol. XII of Marcus Dods' edition): 'The first woman was formed from the side of the man when asleep, and was called Life, and the mother of all living. . . . This Second Adam bowed his head and fell asleep on the cross, that a spouse might be formed for him from that which flowed from the Sleeper's side.' Hoskyns, *The Fourth Gospel, ad. loc.*, quotes another passage from St Augustine, *The City of God*, XXII, 17, to the same effect. Cf. also the lovely sequence for the Feast of Dedication, *Hierusalem et Syon filiae*:

> Blood and water shedding abundantly
> From His riven side He created her,
> On the rood-tree hanging in Calvary
> God Incarnate.
> First of women, Eva had typified
> How His holy Church should be fashionèd,
> Hapless Eva, erst in a mystery
> Formed from Adam.

8. Rev. 19.6–9, 21.1f.

9. Mark 11.1–10; Matt. 21.1–9; Luke 19.29–38; John 12.12–15; Luke 24.50ff.; Acts 1.1–11.

10. St Bernard, *In Dominica Palmarum*, Sermon I.2.

11. John 19.30.

CHAPTER 6. THESE LAST DAYS

1. Heb. 10.12–14. RSV.

2. See Heb. 12.1–13 and 1 Cor. 4.9. In the latter passage 'a spectacle to the world' is in Greek 'a *theatron* to the *cosmos*'—a drama enacted before the universe.

3. Matt. 28.20.

4. Col. 1.24. NEB.

5. See Note 2.

CHAPTER 7. THENCE HE SHALL COME

1. See, for example, St Peter's sermon in Acts 2.14ff., citing Joel 2.28ff.; see also Heb. 1.1f.; 1 Pet. 1.20; 1 John 2.18.

2. Heb. 12.2. NEB.

3. Said by Canon M. R. Newbolt on Good Friday, 1914.

4. C. C. Torrey, *Our Translated Gospels*, pp. 45f.

5. Acts 1.10f.

6. Matt. 25.1–13.

7. Luke 19.11–27.

8. Matt. 25.14–30.

9. Mark 4.26–29.

10. Acts 3.19–21.

11. Luke 18.8. RSV.

CHAPTER 8. THE END OF MAN

1. Mark 9.2–8; Matt. 17.1–8; Luke 9.28–36.

2. 1 Cor. 15.20–22; Rom. 5.12–21; cf. 2 Esd. 7.46–48.

3. John 10.18.

4. In 1 Cor. 15.

5. 2 Thess. 2.8 uses both. For *parousia* alone see Matt. 24.3,27,37,39; 1 Cor. 15.23; 1 Thess. 2.19, 3.13, 4.15, 5.23; 2 Thess. 2.1; Jas. 5.7f.; 2 Pet. 1.16, 3.4 and 12; 1 John 2.28. For *epiphaneia* see 1 Tim. 6.14; 2 Tim. 1.10, 4.1 and 8; Titus 2.13.

6. Mark 8.38; Luke 9.26; Matt. 25.31.

7. See Chapter 6, Note 2.

8. Matt. 25.31–46.

9. 1 Cor. 2.9; Isa. 64.4.

10. Marle Ebner Eschenbach, cited in *World Christian Digest*, March 1953.

11. Rev. 21 and 22.

CHAPTER 9. THE PRACTICE OF EXPECTATION

1. Mark 13.33–37; Matt. 24.42 and 25.13; Luke 21.34–36.

2. Luke 2.22–35; Mal. 3.1.

3. Rev. 3.20.

4. Cassiopeia is on the directly opposite side of the Pole Star from the Plough, and about the same distance from it.

PART II

CHAPTER 10. THE MEANING OF 'CHURCH'

1. See Eph. 2.19–22 and 4.12; 1 Cor. 3.16f.; 2 Cor. 6.16; and 1 Pet. 2.5.

CHAPTER 11. THE GENESIS CREATION NARRATIVES

1. The first letter of this word is the guttural *Aleph*, for which English has no equivalent. Both vowels are broad, and the *d*, following a vowel, has the sound of soft *th*, as in *this*.

2. Cf. wer-wolf = man-wolf. *Wer* is the same as Latin *vir*.

3. St Irenaeus, *Demonstration of the Apostolic Preaching*, tr. J. Armitage Robinson, p. 101.

CHAPTER 12. THE FIRST MAN

1. Luke 3.23–38 and 1.26–35.

2. See, for example, Heb. 4.15, which is really a summing-up of the Gospel story.

3. See C. S. Lewis, *Perelandra*, pp. 227–30.

4. E.g., Hos. 1–3; Jer. 2.2 and 3.14; Isa. 54.5 and 62.5.

5. See Rev. 21 and 22, *passim*.

CHAPTER 13. THE FALL OF MAN

1. 2 Esd. 7.48.

2. St Athanasius, *On the Incarnation of the Word of God*, section 6.

CHAPTER 14. FROM ADAM TO THE FLOOD

1. Through Cain in Gen. 4.16ff.; through Seth in Gen. 5.

2. Gen. 6.9–9.17. Two narratives are interwoven.

CHAPTER 15. THE FIRST CHURCH

1. Gen. 12.1–4. Observe that Abraham was called out in the same two senses as the Greek *ekklēsia* mentioned on p. 59, and like it also was called out to serve the common good.

2. This illustration is borrowed from St Irenaeus, who uses it actually of the obedience of Mary; but of course the principle applies all along the line of preparation for the Incarnation.

3. Gen. 16.

4. D. Nielsen, *Die altarbische Mondreligion*, found in the Bodleian.

5. John 8.56.

6. Gen. 32.

7. 1 Cor. 10.11.

CHAPTER 16. THE SECOND MAN

1. Ecclus. 42.24. AV.

2. Luke 1.38. Mary calls herself *doulē kyriou*; the Servant in Isaiah is of course *doulos*.

3. Luke 1.35.

4. Mark 1.9; cf. Luke 12.50 and Ps. 42.7. Also Luke 11.29f. and Jonah 2.2–9.

5. This ambivalence of water is fundamental, and should be thought about. Consider the fact that it owes its existence to volcanic activity, being formed by the union of the volcanic hydrogen with the free oxygen in the atmosphere. Had the cooling earth not gone through that agony, there could have been no life.

6. Gen. 1.2. The same word is used in Deut. 32.11.

7. The texts recalled by the Father's words in Mark 1.11 are Ps. 2.7 and Isa. 42.1.

8. References for the Baptism and Temptation are Mark 1.9–13; Matt. 3.13–4.11; Luke 3.21f. and 4.1–13.

9. Mark 9.2–8; Matt. 17.1–8; Luke 9.28–36.

10. This is the actual word used in Greek; he was *metamorphosed* before them.

11. Luke 11.21f.

12. 1 Sam. 17. Goliath's demand for a man is in verse 8.

13. It was the late Dr G. A. Cooke, sometime Regius Professor of Hebrew at Oxford, who told me that the whole of this psalm of psalms up to the middle of verse 21 (Prayerbook numbering) could, and indeed should, be taken as retrospective. He was insistent also that the verb in verse 23 is absolute, without an object, and should be translated simply 'that He has acted'.

14. John 19.30.

15. See the Resurrection narratives in all four gospels, and also 1 Cor. 15.3ff.

16. 1 Cor. 15.23.

CHAPTER 17. THE SECOND CHURCH

1. 1 Pet. 3.18ff.

2. That our Lord spent nine months in his mother's womb is implied by Luke 2.6 and emphasised by the dates of Lady Day and Christmas in the Calendar.

3. See Gen. 3.17ff., and cf. Exod. 11.4, and Jonah 3.5ff.; see also Jer. 12.4.

4. Rom. 8.19.

5. Eph. 4.4–13. RSV.

6. Rev. 21.9.

7. See Luke 11.21f.

8. See 1 Cor. 15.35ff.

9. Matt. 25.31–46. The parable implies that all men will be judged on *love*; for all men have the power and the chance of loving.

10. Rev. 21.1f.

11. One may observe that the *ekklēsia* in Noah's Ark included animals.

CHAPTER 18. ON BEING HUMAN

1. Konrad Lorenz, in *King Solomon's Ring: New Light on Animal Ways*.

2. The Plymouth Museum used to have a wonderful specimen of a skeleton in this position, interred in a stone kist, that came from Harlyn Bay in Cornwall; but I do not know if it survived the blitz. The burials still *in situ* at Harlyn Bay are imperfect.

3. Lev. 17.11; cf. Deut. 12.23.

4. C. C. Torrey, *Our Translated Gospels*, pp. 14ff.

INDEX